Out of the Shadows

Teens Write About Surviving Sexual Abuse

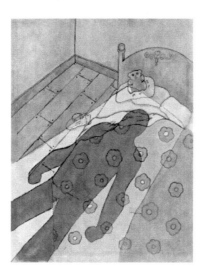

By Youth Communication

Edited by Al Desetta

YOUTH
COMMUNICATION
True Stories by Teens

Out of the Shadows

EXECUTIVE EDITORS
Keith Hefner and Laura Longhine

CONTRIBUTING EDITORS
Rachel Blustain, Nora McCarthy, Laura Longhine, Sheila Feeney, Marie Glancy, Kendra Hurley, and Autumn Spanne

LAYOUT & DESIGN
Efrain Reyes, Jr. and Jeff Faerber

COVER ART
Mariet Guerrero

For reprint information, please contact Youth Communication.

ISBN 978-1-933939-81-0

Second, Expanded Edition
Previous editions of this book were entitled
"Living A Lie" and "Haunted By My Past."

Printed in the United States of America

Youth Communication ®
New York, New York
www.youthcomm.org

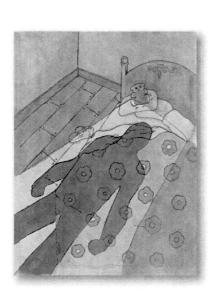

Table of Contents

Contents

Contents

Introduction

Many young people, especially in foster care, have been sexually abused. If you've been a victim of sexual abuse, we hope the stories in this book will encourage you to find a safe place to speak up. As one teen writes, "If one person doesn't believe you, tell someone else. Keep telling until someone listens. I know it's painful to tell, but what you're living with is far worse."

Abusers exert enormous pressure on thier victims to keep the abuse a secret, making victims feel ashamed, guilty, or afraid to speak up. Victims may also have deeply conflicting and confusing feelings about their abuser, especially if it's someone they loved or trusted.

Survivors of sexual abuse need to know that they are not at fault, and they are not alone. This book includes first-person accounts by teen survivors, both male and female. The writers share their feelings of fear, shame, and guilt, as well as how they found the strength to speak up, and the ways they've been able to start healing.

In many of these stories, the trauma of abuse is made worse by family members and other adults who turn a blind eye to the abuse or refuse to believe victims who speak up.

In "I'm Glad I Spoke Up," the author tells several family members that she's being abused, but they either don't believe her or downplay the abuse, telling her to avoid the abuser. The author of "A Partner in His Crime?" is molested by a neighbor for years, but doesn't tell her mother because she fears her mother will blame her. Sure enough, when she finally tells a counselor at school, her mother is angry. "Like I thought would happen, she accused not Johnny, but me," the author writes. "She accused me of liking what Johnny was doing, and said that was why I continued going over there."

Not being believed can be devastating to victims who've found the courage to tell someone the truth. As Dr. Leonard Gries, a mental health expert interviewed in "When Loved Ones Don't Listen" explains:

"Kids who do not feel supported can blame themselves more for the abuse. They also may feel guilty that they've hurt those around them when they spoke up. Not being believed makes them feel further isolated, alone, and powerless."

Fortunately, many of the teens in this book describe how they were able to break through their families' denial and silence, and reach out to other supportive adults. In "Eyes Wide Shut," the author's grandmother becomes angry when the author starts speaking up about the abuse going on in their home. So the author talks to other relatives instead, and escapes the abuse by going into foster care.

In "Making It Out," the author is trapped in a foster home with a cousin who is sexually abusing her, and an aunt who refuses to believe what's happening. But the author finally talks to friends and teachers at school, who believe her and call the cops. "It was like parachuting into the sky, when the detectives believed me over my cousin," she writes. "I felt free."

This book also includes two adult perspectives: from a mother who is devastated to find out that her husband has been abusing their 5-year-old daughter, and from a father who had sexually abused his children and their friends. Both adults had themselves been sexually abused as children, which highlights the importance for victims of getting help to deal with the abuse they experienced. The teen author of "Haunted," a victim of sexual abuse himself, interviewed Nick, the former sex offender, and wrote:

"He made me see that sexual abuse is often perpetrated by people who were themselves victims of sexual abuse—people who can't deal with their own feelings of rage and humiliation, and go and take those feelings out on someone else. He made me look at myself and make sure that I was dealing with my abuse instead of hiding from it."

The final stories and interviews in the book focus on why it's so important to speak up and to find supportive adults who will believe you, and explain how therapy and other supports can help you recover.

In most stories, names and identifying details have been changed.

Note to Readers:
Survival Strategies

When reading this book it is hard not to focus on the abuse and victimization suffered by the writers. But don't let that over-whelm you. The more important message in these stories—and the reason the teens worked so hard to write them—is that in the end they all found a way to stop the abuse and move on toward a happier, healthier place. If you read the stories closely, one thing you'll see is the amazing things these young writers did to escape the abuse and begin to heal. It's true that sometimes people did not listen to them. But they never gave up. Here is just a partial list of all the ways these brave writers reached out for help.

Tell my grandmother and aunt
Tell a school counselor
Talk to the police
Talk with my cousin
Confide in a friend
Go into foster care
Go into a mental hospital
Be open with my social worker, doctor, and therapist
Go on medication
Get an order of protection
Go to counseling with my caregiver
Tell my stepmother
Tell my mother
Tell the staff at my group home
Remember better memories
Interview an abuser
Talk to my mom
Tell my grandmother
Tell my cousin

Tell my caseworker
Write down my thoughts
Recognize my own strengths
Accept genuine love and affection
Accept support from social workers and teachers
Grow close with good male teacher
Get support from other teen survivors
Realize that what I've experienced is just one part of a long life
Go to a psychiatric hospital
Talk in therapy
Send a letter to my mother
Accept the limitations of my mom (to protect or nurture me)
Tell my mom

Out of the Shadows

Tell the police
Go to therapy
Go to therapy again
Write about it
Tell my sister
Talk with my guidance
    counselor
Tell my Spanish teacher
Go to a teen clinic for
    counseling
Go into a good foster home
Accept help from my guidance
    counselor and foster mother
Decide not to blame myself
Realize it's not my fault
Realize that living with abuse is
    more painful than telling
Believe my child
Get a therapist for my child
Stay sober; go to rehab
Tell my mother
Tell the principal
Tell my friends
Tell my aunt
Tell the school dean
Tell the police

Keep busy reading and
    listening to music
Go to therapy
Talk about it only as much as
    I can handle
Write to help others
Make my own choices; take
    more control of my life
Draw
Show my drawings to my
    grandmother
Leave clues for my mother
Talk to my parents
Write and draw in a journal
Verbally confront the abuser
Confide in a teacher with
    poetry
Detach my mind from my body
Get an order of protection
Experiment with relationships
    with a safe person
Acknowledge how far I've
    come and how far there is
    to go
Be self aware about my feelings
    and actions

Edicson Estevez

I'm Glad I Spoke Up

By Anonymous

When I was young, I was scared to go to bed. I knew that as soon as the lights were off, my cousin would come in the room and touch me.

I felt that if I ever told, nobody would believe me. And that was sort of the truth. People are afraid to admit that things like this are happening. Especially if it's someone in the family who's doing the abuse.

When I was about 11, I tried to speak up. I was in the bathroom with my grandmother and my aunt. I told them my cousin had touched me. They didn't believe me because, they said, he was "a good kid." So I lied and said he touched my stomach real hard. I just had to swallow the pain.

When I was about 12, I told a school counselor. I didn't tell him everything, just a few things. One day when my grand-mother took me to school, my counselor spoke to her. After that, I was taken away to the Dominican Republic, where my family is from. My grandmother and I never sat down to talk about what had happened. I felt like I was the one who had done something wrong.

While I was adjusting to a new atmosphere, free of the sexual abuse and making new friends, I felt scared. I mean, what if my cousin was doing it to my little cousins back in New York?

A few months later I was returned to New York City.

My cousin found a girlfriend. The abuse stopped and I learned to forgive him. Not forget, just forgive. We never spoke about it. Nobody in the family did. I was carefree for two years. Then my "uncle" came along.

He was really my cousin's uncle, but I considered him my uncle too. We became good friends, and I trusted him. I told him a lot of secrets about me. I felt he listened. I was wrong to trust him. I felt him look at me in a weird way, but I didn't want to think about that. Not again.

My aunt told me to avoid my uncle. Hello! How could I avoid him in my own home?

My uncle became friend-lier. He was constantly nervous around me. He looked at me as if I were a piece of meat. I grew scared. He hugged me in a weird way. He brushed his beard in my face, and my tears ran down my cheeks.

I was the target, always. I think that's because I'm the one who has a "crackhead mother" and a careless father. But whatever reason made me the target, I knew it wasn't right. I looked for help. I told my aunt. My aunt told me to avoid my uncle. Hello! My uncle was the one who came looking for me. How could I avoid him in my own home?

I thought my aunt would tell my uncle something so that he would stop. But he never stopped. He wrote me a letter. I couldn't believe it. The nerve of this guy. He talked about how good it felt to have sex. About how little girls are doing it too. I didn't want to hear those things and he knew it. I didn't know what to do.

I was cutting school. My grades were so low. I was an honor roll student who went down to the "dropout class." My aunt was constantly screaming at me. I joined a gang. I didn't really do all the bad stuff, but I used to fight a lot and steal little things, like key chains or whatever.

I started to cut myself. Seeing my blood relaxed me. I didn't eat much or sleep much. I dressed real big. I drank pills, but I got so used to it that they didn't cause me any damage. I tried everything to die, but God didn't let me go.

One day my school counselor called me. She couldn't believe my grades. Overwhelmed, I told her everything. She called my house. She spoke to my aunt, who said she knew nothing about it. When I got home, my aunt asked me why I told the counselor.

That night some cops came to my house. They said I had 86 absences from school and there were complaints about me being touched.

My aunt was told to keep my uncle away. I thought things were about to change, but they didn't. My uncle kept coming in and out of the house and touching me. A year after the cops warned my aunt to keep him away I started having nightmares, so I decided to take matters into my own hands. I decided to kill my uncle. I got a friend to lend me his gun.

At home, I wished he would come into the room so I could kill him. I imagined shooting him. I knew it was wrong but I wasn't thinking straight. I saw myself in jail, just like my mother. I saw my family hurting because of me.

One night my little cousin came over to my bed where I was crying. She hugged me and told me not to cry. She burst into tears, next to me. I decided not to touch the gun. I couldn't do it. I gave it back to my friend. He asked if I wanted him to do it for me. That sounded tempting, but I knew it wasn't right.

One day my uncle followed me on the street to school and offered to take me there. Thanks to a friend I saw, he left me alone. That night he came in my room and started to feel up on me. I began to cry and tried to push him away but it was hopeless. I felt his hardness rubbing against me. I felt disgusting, dirty, and hopeless.

That night I stayed up crying. I thought about running away, but I didn't know where to go. I wrote many letters. Good-bye letters. I was going to kill myself once and for all. That was the only way out I saw.

At school I gave one of my best friends a goodbye letter. He started to cry and told a teacher. The teacher told my counselor. My counselor told my psychiatrist, who then called foster care, and I was placed in a hospital's mental ward.

While at first I felt out of place, and all I did was cry, little by little I got better. I had therapy, doctors, social workers, lawyers and so on. They asked me so many questions. I felt I needed some answers, too.

I found out that my little cousins had been taken away from my aunt. I found out that my aunt had finally stood up to the "uncle." My aunt won custody of my little cousins but not me. That was killing me. Everything was happening so fast, and I felt so alone.

I had to trust somebody, so I decided to tell my social worker, my therapist, and my doctor the truth. They put me on medication to help me sort things out. I didn't want to take it but I needed to do things right. That was the only way to get out of there.

In a short time they found me a foster home. It was a nice family and they helped out when I used to feel homesick. They let me call home and go out.

I wanted to be home with my family. It was time for my aunt to prove she was going to take good care of me. But I always felt my aunt didn't love me. While I was in the hospital she told me she loved me, but she had never showed it or protected me. Now it was time for her to show it.

She did pretty well. She got an order of protection to keep my uncle away from me, she attended parenting classes, she went to counselors, she spoke to lawyers and social workers. I was returned to her. It was a trial discharge, to see how things were going to go.

I had to do good also. I had to go to school. This was hard, because I had so much confusion in my head. I was wondering if I had done the right thing by speaking up. I felt I had destroyed the whole family.

I had to wake up at 5 o'clock in the morning and travel one hour just to get to school. That was hard, since I was on medication—I was taking anti-depressants, sleeping pills and another pill to calm my nerves. I had to take my pills and see my doctor

I tried everything to die, but God didn't let me go.

every Saturday. I went to my foster agency regularly. I attended independent living classes. I had to go to court cases on my own. I had to speak to lawyers. I even wrote a letter to the judge.

But it was worth it. I was the student of the month in my school. I was (and still am) admired by my counselors. My aunt and I have a better relationship. We are working on our communication with our counselors and psychologist. My aunt has proven that she does love me. And I feel happy, because she's pretty much like a mother to me. The agency checks on us from time to time. Soon our case will be discharged completely.

I am doing so much better at school and I'm not on medication anymore. I don't get so depressed like before. I still think about my past, but now I think of it as a learning experience. An experience I've survived.

At first I thought that I'd done the wrong thing by speaking up. That's because everyone hated me for it and I felt it was all my fault. But I'm not even mad anymore at those who hated me. They only hated me because I did something that they were scared of. I was strong enough to do it and survive. And I made a difference in everyone who surrounds me.

Now my aunt knows better. My little cousins also know to speak up. They know that it's wrong to be touched and right to stand up for yourself.

Every time I find myself laughing and enjoying life, I know I definitely did the right thing. All the suffering paid off. I know that life isn't a fairy tale, but at least it can get better.

The author was 16 when she wrote this story.

Phillip Rollano

Haunted

By Anonymous

It wasn't my fault. That's what people say. Still, it haunts me every day. I wonder all the time, what did I do that made this happen? Does the fact that I was young mean I couldn't have prevented it? Maybe if I were smarter, I would have understood what was happening. I would not have waited three or four years to tell someone. I could have done something. I didn't stop him. I listened and did what he said. So I'm to blame. Right?

I was 8 years old the day I was molested. It was somewhere between the middle of spring and the middle of summer. It was a regular day. Cats were outside fixing their bikes and messing with firecrackers. I was at my babysitter's house and her son was watching me while she was out.

My babysitter's son was like a role model to me. He was 17, had friends on the block, girls, and was always nice. We would play fight. He'd call me his cousin and take me with him when he went to chill. I was a young boy basically growing up without my father, so he was sort of like a big brother to me.

The day it happened, he and I had just made some burgers and fries and were watching TV. I don't remember if we were talking or what we were watching or really if the TV was even on. I just know I was looking at it. When I was done with my fries I asked him if I could have some more.

He asked me, "You want more fries?" and I said, "Yes, please." So he told me that if I wanted more fries I had to do something. He told me to go in the bedroom and pull down my pants.

I went, only thinking about how I was going to get more French fries. I never have understood why I did what he said and I doubt I ever will. He came in the room and told me to look straight ahead. After that, I don't remember much. I never have been able to recall the pain. I don't even know if there was any. I just assume there was.

After it was over (in my mind it starts and ends at the same time), he gave me some French fries and told me he would kill me if I ever told anyone.

In the weeks after it happened, all I remember is watching Robo Cop and not much else. I think part of the reason I don't remember much is because when something like that happens to you, you don't want to think about it, you just want it to go away, so your mind kind of shuts down. Besides, after it happened, I didn't talk to anybody about it, and when I finally did, they didn't have much to say, so it never seemed that real.

But after it happened, I made up some story to convince my mom to get me a new babysitter. After she did I thought it would be all over, but really, it wasn't. For a couple of years I pushed it out of my mind, but still it haunted me in other ways.

For one, my behavior changed from bad to worse. I was doing everything and anything that could be done with girls,

except for the actual act of sex (my mom '
burn in hell). I got kicked out of school for u
3rd grade. Plus, I started stealing.

My behavior wasn't all about the rape. I was a.
bad boy. But it did make me act even crazier. I acted n.
of wild ways without really knowing why, like I wasn't x.
my own life, like I was on autopilot, like I was watching myse.
on TV.

I never thought about the rape itself. I guess I had blocked it
out so much that I didn't even remember that it happened. But
in little ways it would come up.

I had a toy car that I had
liked to play with which I
had left at my old babysitter's
house, and for years I bugged
my mother about getting it back
from there. It was the car from

After it was over, he gave me some French fries and told me he would kill me if I ever told anyone.

the cartoon *Bionic 5*. It was purple and yellow with missiles. I
had it with me every time I went to that house, and sometimes I
would leave it there. After, I would always think about how I lost
my car in that house and I couldn't go and get it back.

At the time, I didn't understand what I had truly lost, or that
the car was a symbol of something bigger—a symbol of everything that had been taken from me when my babysitter's son
raped me. I just knew it was important and that I longed to have
it back.

Then, when I was 10, I was just sitting down one day and
everything flashed through my head and I realized I had been
molested and that I needed to tell someone. I thought about
everything I had done with girls and felt ashamed, because they
hadn't fully understood what we had been doing anymore than I
had. I felt I had become like him, my babysitter's son.

By then I was living down south with my father, so I went to
tell my stepmother. I was scared, but I thought that since she was
a psychiatrist she could make it go away. But all she said was that

.vasn't my fault and then she let it drop. I left feeling even more onfused. I felt dumb for even bringing it up.

Then when I was 11 and living with my mom again, I told her what had happened. I had begun to have a lot of flashbacks of the rape and I could tell that my mom was worried. But when I told her, she and her boyfriend acted like I didn't tell them anything at all. I understood that it was four or five years after it happened, but she didn't even hug me.

She just said, "What you want me to do about it? It's too late now. You should have told me when it happened." I went to my room and cried. I felt that it must have been my fault if no one could or would help me.

I walk around with a secret I feel I have to hide. I know that lots of girls who have been molested feel that way too. But maybe guys feel it even more.

Soon I was thinking about it every day. I could just be walking and I'd remember it. It really didn't take anything. The worst was when I was 15. By then I had entered the foster care system, and I got into a scrape with three or four guys in my group home who started rumors that I was gay.

Every day I was approached by someone who had heard the rumors. I was afraid to go to sleep because one or two kids said they were going to sneak into my room and have sex with me. I had to fight people off and on until the whole thing died down. I was in a constant state of turmoil.

And in the background, always, there was my secret. Every day I would wonder, "Can people tell I was molested? Do I walk like regular cats or do people see a 'take advantage' sign on me?" I wondered, "Am I gay because some man molested me when I was 8?" After all, I took my pants off when he asked me to, didn't run when he did it. I was afraid it was my fault, that it was something I had wanted, something I made happen.

Even after the rumors died down, I continued to try to prove I was a man. I looked for trouble in the streets and talked to anything with a pretty face. I once hopped out of a car to get a girl's number because my uncle said she looked like something I should bag. But none of that made my fears go away.

Instead, the memories came back with a vengeance. Last year, I was bugging out about something or other and staff restrained me. I started to get the signs I usually get before a flashback—which is when memories of that time come flooding back as if they were happening right then. I tried to get in control, but it was too hard with two guys holding me down. I started catching little spasms, so they held me tighter.

I tried to tell them to let go. I told them anything that came to mind. The staff wouldn't listen, and after a while I just remembered so much that happened that day I was 8 and started shaking. Next thing I knew I was crying. I wasn't totally out of control yet, so I turned my head so they wouldn't notice. I was afraid that if the staff knew I had been molested, they would go and spread my business and crack jokes.

Finally, it all happened at once. The tears were running down my face and I was shouting, "You're not going to do that stuff again" and trying to fight them off of me. The staff called for an extra hand. One was at my feet and legs, one was sitting on my back, and one was pulling my wrist to my shoulder. Finally, I calmed myself down.

I told the staff to close the door and I told them what had happened. I felt pitiful. I was afraid to look the staff in the eye. I didn't want to tell them what had happened. The last nine years had taught me that it was better to hide it.

Nothing much happened, though, good or bad. The staff were cool. They got up and said they were sorry. I told them I understood they had to do their job, and that was that.

I still think about what happened almost every day. I walk around with a secret that I feel I have to hide. I know that lots of girls who have been molested feel that way too. But maybe guys feel it even more—like it has to be hidden so deep, like we have to hide it even from ourselves. If my parents had sat me down and talked to me instead of acting like it never happened, maybe I would feel less ashamed.

The feelings I've had all these years are so strong. I never saw my baby-sitter's son after my mom took me to a new one. I don't remember his name, and I doubt I would recognize his face. But once when I was 13, I tried to find him because I wanted to kill him. The thought filled my head every day for about three months. But I was too afraid to walk down that block where he lived.

Last summer I'd had a little to drink and I guess the liquor gave me the courage to confront my demons, so I decided to go there. I had stopped being afraid of seeing my babysitter's son. I was just afraid of the pain I might feel from the memories of the rape.

But when I got to that block, I recalled other sorts of memories, good memories—my kindergarten graduation, old friends and family who used to live there too. It gave me a type of release to confront my fears. And so has writing this story. Life's got a screwed up sense of humor, but I guess I think that if I deal with the scars, one day they might heal.

Still, there's a part of me that doesn't know if I can ever fully deal with the rape. It always makes me wonder if someone's trying to take advantage of me. It makes me feel I've got a shameful thing I have to hide.

It's messed up that something that happened when I was 8 can still affect me so much now. It's messed up that someone can come into your life for so brief a time and screw everything up so much. I feel like no matter what I do, I can't get back what was stolen. But I'm writing this story because I also know that if I keep it hidden from myself, the abuse will only surface in more painful ways.

The author was 19 when he wrote this and the following story.
He later joined the Marines and ran a computer business.

Phillip Rollano

'I'm Sorry':
A Sex Offender Speaks Out

By Anonymous

"When I tell this, I am full of shame. I am full of guilt. I am horrified. I don't know how to live with it, but I've found that the best way to live with it is to be honest about it."

These are the words of a former sex offender who I interviewed, a man who molested his children and his children's friends.

I interviewed him after I wrote *Haunted*, the previous story in this book. My editor suggested I talk to a sex offender. I thought it might be therapeutic for me, and it was.

Still, it was scary for me to interview him, sort of like meeting my worst fear face to face. I thought that it was going to be one of the most horrible experiences of my life. I thought I was going to bug out and just flip on the guy. I didn't know what to expect because I really had a hatred toward people like him. But what happened was very different.

Nick was not the demonic person I imagined. He didn't seem like "one of those," a child molester. He was actually very sorry for what he did and was trying to prevent it from ever happening again. I was almost moved to tears because I felt bad for all the hatred I had felt toward him in the beginning. At the end, as strange as it sounds, I felt that we shared a lot of common ground.

I was able to understand his feelings of hopelessness. He made me see that sexual abuse is often perpetrated by people who were themselves victims of sexual abuse—people who can't deal with their own feelings of rage and humiliation, and go and take those feelings out on someone else. He made me look at myself and make sure that I was dealing with my abuse instead of hiding from it, because I would never want to do to someone else what was done to me. Abuse as a whole continues in cycles. Nick made me see that I needed to make sure that the cycle didn't continue with me.

At the same time, it was confusing to me because I still have so much hatred for the guy who raped me. And really, I think I should. At least Nick has come out and admitted what he's done. He's said he understands if his kids never want to talk to him again (although some of them do). He's trying to do his part to make sure others get the help they need.

But lots of people don't do that. Nick said himself that when he was in jail, he talked to a lot of guys who had sexually abused young kids, and some of them didn't even think what they did was wrong. That just makes me so angry. In fact, sometimes it makes me so angry that I really feel like I could kill.

But even though I've still got all my rage at the guy who raped me, it felt good for me to finally have some glimpse into "their" minds. It helped me see that the people who do this have problems, and that the victims are, at least to some extent, faceless to them. They stop being real people and become just something the person can touch. And that realization helped me see that it wasn't my fault and that I wasn't the reason it happened.

Since the interview, the daily flashbacks I used to have—when I remembered the day I was raped as if it was happening right then—have stopped.

When I talked to Nick, I was able to feel his guilt and his sorrow so deeply that I knew it couldn't be just a show. He is a man who is trying the only way he knows how to correct his past mistakes—by talking about them.

So here is Nick, a sex offender, describing his experience, in his own words:

Nick's Story

I don't know if I know enough to generalize about what motivates abusers, but I can tell you a little about my own situation if that's helpful to you. It's difficult to explain. I have to grope and reach to put the words together.

When I was a child, I was sexually abused by my father. I wanted his love and companionship, I just didn't want the touching. But I didn't want to lose the relationship I had with him either, so I didn't tell him to stop.

Instead, I found another way to escape. When I was a child being abused, I would feel myself floating up to the ceiling. It let me go out of my body and detach my emotions. I don't know, but I think maybe that experience is a little bit like what happened when I reached out and touched the children I touched.

I was an adult with a family of my own when I began to abuse my children and other children. Before I did it, I found I was fantasizing a lot about having sexual contact. But the more I thought about sex, and as my interest became more focused, the person became not a person. They became more of an idea, just a thing to touch.

I was married and I had eight children, five girls and three boys. My children have told me that I was hostile and aggressive and angry all the time. I was too powerful and I was pushing myself around. And even though there were some good times, I created an environment that was a nightmare, a terror, and they dreaded me coming home.

Then I started the sexual abuse. The victims were almost all my own children, and two of my daughters' girlfriends. They were around the age of 14 or 15.

I would look in their bedroom at night to check that they were in bed, like I had since they were little girls. Then I began to fondle them. I would tell myself, "This is certainly something I don't want to do. I won't ever do it again." Then I would start thinking about body parts again, and I would get excited. I realized I had a problem, but part of me just shut down and denied it. I was very scared that if I was found out I would lose my position and my family, that my mask would be taken away and I would have to admit what I had done wrong to the ones I had abused.

Then one of my daughters went to her godfather and told him what had been happening. He said, "I've known Nick a long time and I don't believe he would do that. But if it's true, let's go talk to him about it." My daughter said she wanted to deal with it herself. But he said he would only give her a short time. Otherwise, his conscience and his manhood mandated that he go talk to me.

Eventually he came up to me and asked, "Nick, have you been sexually molesting your daughters?" And I said, "What are you talking about?" He said, "Nick, I'm sorry to have to ask you this as a friend, but have you been sexually molesting your daughters?" And I said, "Yes, I have."

It was shocking to me and it was shocking to him. We were both afraid of what might happen, that there might be a violent blow up. I suggested I call my wife and let her know what had happened, and tell her it was my fault and not the children's fault.

After that, he was supportive, understanding, firm. Before he talked to me, he had called a lawyer and asked him if it would be best if I was incarcerated for the safety of the community. He also didn't know if I might commit suicide.

First, I had to deal with the fact that I had been abused myself. Then I needed to deal with what I had done.

That was something I thought about myself. I thought it might be the best thing if I killed myself if that's what it took to make the world safe. All of my family pleaded with me and they said that whatever I had done, it would be far worse if I killed myself, because then they would have to deal with that too.

We went to family therapy and then I turned myself into the district attorney. I said, "Here I am," and he said, "You should go talk to a lawyer." And I said, "I won't do that. I won't put myself up against my family. Put an end to it," and I went to jail.

When I went to jail, I was shocked. There were about 100 people in my wing, and about 85 out of 100 admitted to me that they had been involved in child sexual abuse. Of those people, some were very motivated to change and very aware, some were still in denial, and some didn't think what they did was wrong. Those were the people who really horrified me.

I did want to change, and for me group therapy helped. Talking about what happened was like coming back alive again, it was like coming out of the closet, becoming a real person rather than a fake. I was alive rather than dead and dying. I was filled with hope rather than a nightmare. I couldn't correct what had happened in the past, but I could set guidelines to prevent it in the future.

First, I had to deal with the fact that I had been abused myself. The hardest thing to accept is that it really did happen. You want to say, "No, no, no." But I couldn't heal until I had accepted that I had experienced it. Someone else can shoot a rifle, but if it hits me, I still have to heal.

Then I needed to deal with what I had done. By sharing our stories in group therapy, we saw patterns to watch out for. For instance, if I'm in a cycle and I'm depressed and angry, and then I start drinking and drugging, and then I start fantasizing, I have to stop myself, or pick up the phone and call my therapist or call a friend, and say, "Something is wrong."

Some of my children opted not to talk to me, and some were prevented by a restraining order. Still, I was grateful that some of my children were willing to.

Four out of eight of them have made contact with me since that time and they've told me that they're glad I'm living honestly, they're glad I'm in therapy. I've done some public speaking now about being a sexual abuser and they're very supportive of that work. I think they would have been horrified irrevocably and filled with hatred if I had not been honest and open.

They've been to therapy too. One of them is a teacher and, like me, she made the decision to talk openly with other people about the abuse. She's said that coming through that experience and being able to come to terms with it has made her a better teacher, and has allowed her to empathize with her students more. She's still in school and she's writing her thesis on this, and she's asked me to go over it with her. I feel honored that she wants me to.

When my father abused me, part of me hated him and wanted to beat him up, and part of me loved him. The fact that I felt love for him was incomprehensible to me. He only died a year or so ago, but when I confronted him about the abuse he refused to talk about it, so I had to find other ways of coming to terms with it.

For a long time, I thought about getting revenge on my father. Partly it was a macho thing, partly it was a question of sheer revenge. But I had to realize that he was the person who was sick and troubled and that I didn't do anything wrong. It was his problem. It was important to get rid of that guilt that I participated in it, even unwillingly, even if I couldn't control it. When I realized that what he did was wrong, I could move on and let go, instead of being tied up hating the person. I had to let it go and take care of me.

Talking about what happened was like becoming a real person. I was alive rather than dead and dying. I was filled with hope rather than a nightmare.

If I had to say one thing to a victim, I would say, "I'm so sorry for what I did. Me, I did it. It's not your fault. I was the one who was wrong. Don't attack yourself. Attack what I did. I know I can never make it up to you, but I'm going to show you that I'm trying to change."

And I would say, "You need to get help for yourself, not from me, from others, but get help. If I had gotten help earlier, I don't think I would have done as much abuse as I did."

—Nick

Rosa Perin

Eyes Wide Shut

By Anonymous

"Drip, drop. Tears of sorrow began to fall from my dejected face, full of endless horror and shame. No more could I take seeing or hearing each fist thrown rapidly at my mother. While hearing my mother's cries, I felt as if I were her, crying and feeling each fist being pounded right into her as if it were me."

These are words that I wrote in my journal, explaining the agony I felt through my childhood years. My father came back into my life when I was 6, but he wasn't much of a dad to me.

My father had a mental illness and he would beat us a couple of times a week. He would hit me, he said, because I was not as pretty as my twin sister and because he wanted one child, not two. He would also sexually abuse me.

I saw my mom and sister getting hit, cursed, and sexually

abused, too. Usually I saw this all through a little hole in the floor of my bedroom. I felt so helpless. I didn't know what to do to stop my own suffering, or to stop the suffering of my mother and sister.

Once I noticed cuts on my sister's wrists. When I asked her, she told me she had done it to herself. It took a while before she told me why she did it. She did it because she thought the pain from the cuts would make her forget the pain in her heart. That night I couldn't sleep. All I could do was cry.

Every day coming home from school I'd think about how I wanted to find another family or just disappear, but there was no other place for me to go.

Other times I wanted to fight back, but I didn't have enough power. Once when I was 7, my father came racing into the room and picked up my sister and pulled down her pants and underwear. When I saw the tears coming from my sister's eyes, I ran and jumped on my father's back and I bit him on his neck. After that he banged my head against the wall and slapped me really hard repeatedly. I wanted to fight him so badly and make him stop, but I knew I was too weak. I knew this was Daddy and more was to come.

For many years, I felt like I needed to find a way out of the hell I was in. But no one in my family seemed to be doing anything to change the situation.

My mother suffers from depression. Maybe it's because during her childhood her father abused her, too. Even before our father came back into our lives, my mother was always quiet. Sometimes she would sit at the table and stare out the window for hours.

So when my father started abusing us, I really didn't expect much help from my mom. Sometimes I felt angry at her anyway. I didn't understand why she would marry someone she was afraid of, and I was angry that she would stay with someone who hurt me. Sometimes I would yell at her, "You don't have to take this," or, "Get a divorce."

One day in school the kids started teasing me. There were rumors going around that my dad was raping and beating his family. The thing that made me really sad was that the rumors were true. That day, I tried again to talk to my mom about it. She denied everything.

I knew my mom was listening somewhere inside of her, but although my mom was older and bigger than I was, I realized that she just wasn't strong enough to help herself or us. She was scared and confused, which made me feel scared and confused. It also made me feel so sad for her, and I wished and hoped that both of us could be happier.

I remember one day, when my father wasn't home, sitting and looking out the window with my mom. That was the time I remember being most happy, because everything was at peace. That day I knew my mom and I both wanted to break free. Finding a way out was the hard part.

I wanted to know why my grandmother didn't do anything to protect us. Soon she was calling me a problem child, a liar, and a bad person.

Luckily, I had my grandmother in my life. My father's mother was really more of a mother to me than my own mother. She was that strong and brave person I could look up to. She was active and energetic, and had a good job in real estate that she would sometimes take me to. She acted like she wasn't going to let anything stand in the way of her being happy.

She lived with us also and I slept in bed with her at night. We'd watch movies and game shows like *Jeopardy* and *Wheel of Fortune* together. I would talk to her if I had a crush on a boy, and any questions I had about puberty she would answer. We'd go jogging in the park and shopping. Being around my grandma made me feel safe and happy.

My grandmother witnessed at least some of the things my

father did to my mother, my sister, and me, and she tried to talk to her son, but he ignored her. Instead, my grandma tried to get my sister and me out of the house to have fun. We'd go to the beach and to the mall.

Sometimes, though, I felt angry at my grandmother because none of that was enough to protect us from my father. Sometimes out of the blue my grandmother would say, "You have to get out of here," or "You should go to foster care," but then she'd drop it.

Usually I was able to force any anger I felt at my grandmother out of my heart and mind. I knew my grandmother had deep love for her son, but that did not seem like a good enough reason for why she didn't protect me. So instead I just tried not to think about it, because the more I thought about it the angrier I got. I didn't want to be angry at my grandmother. I didn't want to lose the relationship we shared, because no one else was giving me the kind of love that she was.

But then one night my sister and I were at my other grandmother's hanging out with my cousin. My cousin was talking about how sometimes her parents hit her, and I felt like I couldn't hold my secrets in any longer. I guess she saw me looking sad because she said to me, "What's wrong? Tell me." It took me a while to get it all out but I finally told her. I told about my father hitting, cursing, and sexually abusing us. When my cousin asked me a question, I answered it, although there were some things that my father did that hurt too much. Those I kept secret.

I told her because I felt comfortable with her. She told me that she wouldn't tell anyone else and I chose to believe her, because then I wouldn't have to be so scared of the consequences. But inside, I think I knew that if my cousin really cared she would tell someone.

The whole time I was talking my sister was very quiet. I knew she might be upset with me in the moment, but I also knew she'd be happier in the end if we didn't have to go through the abuse anymore, so I kept talking. While I talked, my cousin began to cry. In a way I felt happy when I saw her tears, because I knew it meant she cared about me.

She told me that I should tell my grandma (my mother's mother), and that she would understand because she loved me. I told her I didn't think that I was ready. Later, though, I found out that when she went home she told her father, and he talked to my grandma, and they decided that something had to be done.

A couple of weeks after that the phone rang and my father picked it up. It was my grandma, asking if he had been sexually abusing us. I didn't know that at the time. I just heard him say, "No, no," and then he hung up quickly. Next he turned to me, then to my sister, and then to me again and said, "You won't break this family up." Then he rushed out of the room. I realized then that he knew I'd told, and I was scared. I was also surprised and relieved that he hadn't hit me for telling.

My father must have told his mother about the telephone call, because after that she began to act angry toward me. One day I was talking to my sister and I was feeling angry, so I said that my grandmother knew what was going on with my father and never did anything about it. My grandmother overheard those words and she called me a liar.

For a moment I thought maybe she hadn't known. But really I knew she knew. Then I felt shocked that my grandmother would lie, because I always thought I could trust her.

After that, I began to get more and more upset and angry. I wanted to know why she didn't do anything to protect us. Soon she was calling me a problem child, a liar, and a bad person all the time. That made me feel so sad, and part of me felt I was to blame that our relationship was gone.

A few weeks later two caseworkers came to my house. I was nervous, but when they questioned me I just told the truth because that's what they told me to do.

Then they questioned other members of my family while I

packed my clothes. My father came in while I was packing. He was shouting and cursing. My grandmother had to calm him down.

While we were packing, my sister told me she was happy to leave but also scared because she didn't know where we were going. I felt scared, just like my sister, but I also felt good, because I knew that wherever I was going, it was better than home.

When I finished packing, I noticed my grandmother looking upset. She wouldn't look at me or speak to me. I felt sad and responsible for making her upset.

If she loved me, she would have realized I had to report what my father was doing.

My father was also sitting there. Something was telling me to say good-bye to him, even though I didn't want to. The voice in my head was saying, "He's still your father and he's sad." I remembered some good times we had had together, like the times we went to the park, and I felt like part of him still deeply loved my sister and me.

I went up to him. He was sitting on the chair with his head down and looked up when I came over. Before I could say good-bye he looked at me straight in my eyes (a look I will never forget) and said calmly, "I guess I'll see you later." He didn't sound angry at all.

I turned and left and didn't look back. I was surprised he didn't yell or act up. I guess he knew he had to face the consequences of hurting the ones he loved.

My sister and I lived in a group home for a few weeks, and then we went to live in my maternal grandmother's house, where I live now. My aunt (my mother's sister) helped my mom get custody of us by offering to be our supervisor. And for the first year or so of living with my grandmother, my aunt took us places, like to a youth group every Sunday, and acted like a second mom. It makes me happy to know I have her love. But recently she's had some problems in her life and sometimes she isn't there for us quite as much.

My dad was put in jail for about four months. Now that he's out, he calls my mom on and off, apologizing and asking to see us. He lives a few blocks from my mom and he tries to speak to her. Sometimes, though, he gets mad and curses at her, which makes me think he hasn't changed. Luckily my mom never responds.

My life has changed a lot since we got away from my father. I see that I have strengths I never knew about. For instance, I needed a way to release my anger at my father, and that led me to writing my thoughts and poems. Those poems express the things I feel most deeply. And writing this story lets me help other kids.

I've also come to see the strength I had to speak up about the abuse. My grandmother and aunt say it was a brave thing I did. That makes me feel happy. The caseworkers were really nice, too, and told me what I did was brave. I think they're right. I

My life has changed a lot since we got away from my father. I see that I have strengths I never knew about.

feel particularly good when my sister tells me how happy she is that we are gone from that situation. All that love and affirmation has made it easier for me to come to terms with the trauma. I feel like I've been able to let go of a lot of the pain.

Of course, there are many ways that the abuse still affects me. I'm very shy and insecure around other kids because I'm still affected by all the negative things my father said to me. But the one thing that makes me the saddest is that when I spoke up, I lost the relationship that meant the most to me.

After we left her house, my father's mother never called to ask how I was doing. She never visited. She gave away the possessions I left in her home to my cousins. Part of me felt like maybe I was to blame, that maybe I was a bad person. That feeling was strong for a few months and I cried about it every day.

Even though my grandmother was mad at me and I was mad

at her, our relationship is what kept me strong when my father put me down. I wanted her to realize it wasn't my fault. I wanted to speak to her about it, but I couldn't stand her yelling at me. The thought of it made me feel so bad inside. So I waited for her to talk to me, but she never did.

About half a year after we moved out of her house, my grandmother died of cancer. I didn't cry as much as the rest of the family because after a few months of silence, when I realized she wasn't planning to play a role in my life, I began to block her out of my heart. After she died I felt angry that she never made peace with me. I felt so sad, but I tried to let it go. I loved her, but I told myself that if she loved me she would have realized I had to report what my father was doing, so I would stop being hurt.

But it's not so easy to let those feelings go. I still cry many nights because the one person who gave me the most love and support also gave up on me. I still wish for her hugs of warmth. She made me feel that being with her was the only way to be safe.

Having my grandma die without making peace makes me afraid to get too close to anyone. I still make friends and talk to people, but I always have this worry that they're going to leave me. I felt scared and alone growing up, and my grandma was the only person I had to rely on. Now I feel the only person I can really rely on is me.

I wish I had never lost my grandma. It still hurts so much that she rejected me, and I wish someone could have helped us be a family again. But I'm also glad I spoke up because I don't think I could have kept on living with all that pain. My life is much better now than it would have been. And that lets me believe that life can get better still.

The author wrote this story and the following one when she was 14. She later graduated from high school and went on to college, majoring in social work.

When Loved Ones Don't Listen

By Anonymous

"I don't believe you."

"It's your fault."

"You betrayed our family."

Unfortunately, it's not uncommon for teens to hear these words when they finally tell their families that a friend or relative has sexually abused them. What they want is to let out the thoughts that have been haunting them for so long, and to be protected from the abuser so that they can feel some relief. But when kids are rejected or not believed, it feels like there's no use trying to escape the abuse.

It hurts, too, when the people who raised you see the abuse with their own eyes and do nothing.

When my father was being abusive, and neither my mother nor my grandmother nor my extended family (who I always felt must have known some of what was going on) did anything to stop him, everything felt so useless. I just tried to find ways to make my life better while living with the abuse, like going out a lot or doing well in school. Still, the feeling that the people who loved me didn't protect me made me so sad that I cried constantly.

If it hurts a child so much not to be believed or protected, why might a parent or caretaker—sometimes a person who loves you and who you love—react like that?

Sometimes it's because the person who raised you and who loves you also loves the person who abused you. The abuser might be her spouse, partner, uncle or cousin, explained Dr. Mel Schneiderman, the chief psychologist at New York Foundling, a foster care agency. Dr. Schneiderman also said that parents might feel so horrible at the thought that their child was abused, and so guilty for not protecting their child, that instead they just deny the possibility that their child is telling the truth.

Dr. Leonard Gries, head of mental health services at St. Christopher-Ottilie, another foster care agency, added that some parents may have experienced sexual abuse themselves and they never had a chance to deal with it. This may make it harder for them to accept it when their child brings it up.

After I spoke up about the abuse, the hardest part was that my grandmother refused to speak to me.

Whatever the reasons, the consequences can be serious. Not all victims of sexual abuse react the same way, but kids who are not believed tend to suffer more than children who receive support.

"Kids who do not feel supported can blame themselves more for the abuse. They also may feel guilty that they've hurt those around them when they spoke up. Not being believed makes them feel further isolated, alone and powerless," Dr. Gries said.

After I spoke up about the abuse, the hardest part was that my grandmother refused to speak to me. When my grandmother and I had argued in the past, I would just give her a few days to cool off. Then when I saw she was in a good mood, I'd sit on her bed and talk. But after I spoke up about the abuse, her anger made me feel like I had made a terrible mistake, and that I was hurting the person I loved the most.

Not being accepted or believed can sometimes lead to serious psychological problems. "When a child is not believed, that child may begin to doubt herself and her perceptions," said Dr. Schneiderman. Children who do not receive support are more likely to experience severe anxiety, flashbacks, and even more extreme emotional breakdowns.

The support I got from my social workers and teachers helped me stop feeling guilty and made me think less negatively about the world.

Both Dr. Schneiderman and Dr. Gries said that, with proper counseling, many parents who at first didn't believe their child, can accept that what their child is saying.

That's why they said it's important for the foster care system to try to help parents. Dr. Schneiderman said they try to teach parents about sexual abuse. They also talk about how important it is for parents to support their child, and help them work through some of their own issues that might keep them from accepting that their child has been sexually abused.

He also said that it can be very helpful to have parents of sexually abused children together in a group. "When other parents are acknowledging what has happened to their child, sometimes it helps the parent who is not" to acknowledge it.

I really wish someone had been able to help my grandmother and me deal with the anger and hurt between us, but no one did.

Unfortunately, Dr. Schneiderman and Dr. Gries agree that often, even with counseling, parents just won't accept what their child is saying. When that feeling of loss and rejection is severe, that child may carry around a deep feeling of hurt her whole life. When I was little, my grandmother was the one who made me feel like a princess when my whole world felt like a monster. There will always be a place inside me that hurts because in the end she chose her son over protecting me.

Luckily, Dr. Gries found a silver lining in all this bad news. When he conducted a study of close to 30 teens in foster care who had been sexually abused, he found that even when the people who raised them didn't believe and support them, if their foster parents did, they tended to recover better from the trauma of the abuse.

Dr. Gries said that the young people who had foster parents who believed them when they talked about the abuse, who gave them emotional support, and who made sure they received the medical and psychological care they needed, reported feeling less depressed. They also tended to be more comfortable in social situations.

He said that the research made him see just how important it is for foster parents to have training to learn how to care for children who have been sexually abused.

I know from experience that even support from people you don't live with can make a big difference. The support I got from people like my social workers and teachers helped me stop feeling guilty and made me think less negatively about the world. Growing close to one of my male teachers also helped me realize that not all men are scary.

For me, it was also important to get support from other teens, the ones who wrote about their experiences in this book. That, as much as anything else, helped me overcome my shame, because it let me know that I was not alone.

When you receive support to deal with what you've suffered and praise for speaking up, it makes you feel like life is a long road and that what you've experienced is just one of many struggles you'll be able to get through. That support is not magic and it doesn't make all the hurt and shame go away, but it can help you do the work you need to do to come to terms with your past. When you do that, you do feel braver and more free.

The author wrote this story and the previous one when she was 14. She later graduated from high school and went on to college, majoring in social work.

Patricia Battles

Not Yet

By T. Mahdi

I want to talk to my mom again because I want her to be the mom I always dreamed of, the one who would give me attention and listen to me.

I want to hear her tell me that she's proud that I spoke up about my dad sexually abusing my sister and me, even though it meant that we went into foster care. But I don't know if that talk will ever happen.

Last year I was in a psychiatric hospital for several months. When my mom found out, she contacted my social workers and they asked me if I was ready to see her. I was nervous because I hadn't seen my mom in two years. When I'd spoken to her back then about the abuse, she was angry with me and refused to believe my story.

I said I was ready for her visit, but I knew deep down that my mind was going to have a major meltdown.

Then I saw her: short, round and, dark, she matched her coat. It was like seeing a ghost. My therapist said, "Are you ready?" I wanted to say something but my mom looked at me with a look that said, "You are ready." So we went upstairs and I sat across from her.

"Well, there are some things I want to say," my therapist said. She asked my mother, "What made you want to come and see your daughter?"

"Because I love her so much," my mom said.

Part of me wanted to hug her and part wanted to throw a chair at her because I was sure she was lying. She sounded like me—sarcastic. I wanted to tell her every way she'd hurt me. "Why did you give my sister more attention than me?" I asked.

"I didn't," she said. "I gave it all to you because you were always so sick."

I still wanted my mother to acknowledge what happened in our family.

I felt she would never be able to listen without rejecting my version of events. Then the social workers began to talk with my mother. I didn't listen. I was happy and sad at the same time because I felt sure that when she left I would hear more voices and see more hallucinations. It was just too stressful.

"What made you come to the hospital?" my mother asked.

"I cut myself," I told her. She wanted to see my arm. I took it out and she held it like she thought I was lying and had to see it to believe it. My mother took out a small bottle and put lotion on my arm like I hadn't thought of it.

"It's not worth it," she said. "Don't do it again, OK?"

I said OK and she let go.

I was so confused. She says mean things about me and now she's putting lotion on my arm? I stopped listening again. Time went by slowly and when it was over we said our goodbyes and we separated.

After that I had bad flashbacks. I heard my father's voice and had terrible feelings and memories, like of his body lying beside me, and then I cut myself again.

I didn't hear from my mother for two years after that. Then I decided to send a letter to my mother because I still wanted her to acknowledge what happened in our family. The letter said things like, "Did you know about the abuse?" I also asked about her mental illness, because I fear I've inherited it.

Five months later she sent back a letter. I went to my social worker's office to read it. I felt kind of nervous holding it in my hand. I expected that this would be the letter that would tell me if she believed what I said happened. But I as I read it, I felt disappointed.

Other than saying she loved my sister and me, she just kept saying, "I don't know how it could've happened." And, "I don't know where it happened." I thought, "Hello, you were there. Or were you too stoned to realize it?"

I was sad and angry. I kept thinking, "I hate you, I wish you would die." I wanted to scream, but instead I smiled and left the room. At that moment, I decided I just wanted my mother to leave me alone. I'd had enough of her garbage.

But a few weeks ago my social worker came for a visit. She said she had a big surprise. I sat in my room on the floor waiting to hear about the "big surprise." I thought we won the lottery or were going on a trip. Or I feared my mother was sick.

The social worker said, "Here's the surprise: your mother contacted us. She wants to meet with you." I kept on smiling, looking stupid, even though I felt scared and upset inside. I thought, "Why now? You didn't want to see us in the past, so why now?"

At first I thought I would talk to her. Maybe this time she would admit the abuse did happen, and that she had to accept it if she wanted a relationship with my sister and me.

But then I decided not to. I didn't want to get my hopes up and get let down again. That really messes me up.

I imagine I might have an "associate" relationship with my mother one day, if she ever faced reality. But it also might be impossible. I might never agree to see her, and she might never have a change of heart.

The author was 19 when she wrote this story.
She went to college and has won awards
for her writing on mental health issues.

Edwin Yang

Alone With My Abuser

By Anonymous

My hands are icy cold, yet sweaty. The hairs on the back of my neck stand upright like soldiers in salute. I'm so nauseous and dizzy that the room twirls and twirls.

"Turn around, you know you want to. You know you like this."

In the mirror I see a naked 50-year-old man masturbating behind me. I glance at the clock. It seems as if the second hand has frozen, but I can still hear its ticking taunting me, laughing at my assailable heart.

An eternity later, I see a white substance oozing between the cracks on the floor. The stench of his orange body oil is suffocating.

Then: "Oh my God, I'm so sorry. I didn't mean to. I don't know what I was thinking. Please forgive me," he says.

I cry onto his shoulder and let his fingertips caress my hair. I am 12 years old and full of anger, shame, and pity. I pull my head up and scrutinize the brown eyes of my stepfather.

When I was 4, my mom met John in the diner where she worked. They started dating and two years later, when she got pregnant with my sister Vicky, he came to live with us. My stepfather was like a father to me and never treated me as less of a daughter than Vicky. He listened to my stories and told me jokes to cheer me up when I was sad. He helped me with my homework. Once, when I was in 5th grade, he stayed up the whole night building a tower of straws for my school's contest. It broke when I got there, but I still won second place.

My stepfather was like my best friend. That's why I didn't tell anyone what happened that day. I was afraid to lose him. I believed that if I ignored it, then it would be like it never happened.

I also didn't want to risk my mom's marriage. They had just gotten legally married after eight years, and my mom was busy trying to save money to have her long-awaited church wedding. Most of all, I convinced myself not to say anything for the sake of Vicky, who was 6. If my mom left my stepfather, Vicky would grow up without a dad.

I thought that if I ignored him he would eventually stop. I was wrong.

Besides, my stepfather had just lost his job and was depressed. I didn't think it would happen again. That night as my mom, Vicky, my stepfather, and I sat around the table eating dinner, I laughed and talked as if nothing was wrong.

But it didn't stop. My stepfather began touching himself and staring at me nearly every day. Every time, I just stayed still, clenched my teeth and waited until he was finished. I thought that if I ignored him he would eventually stop. I was wrong.

After a while he even stopped apologizing and got spiteful.

He would write me letters saying that I was the devil's child and that I seduced him. He left sticky-notes in front of the computer with phrases like "You're a whore" and, "You know you have fantasies about me." Then he would tear them into tiny pieces and throw them away before my mom got home. Once he even sent me an email saying it was my fault he was doing all this and that I would go to hell.

I didn't understand until much later that besides being sexually abused, I was also being verbally and emotionally abused. Looking back, I feel it was the notes that affected me even more than the sexual abuse. They made me feel guilty, dirty, and ashamed. I let the abuse continue because he made me feel like I deserved it.

When my mom was home, he acted normal, which confused me and made me feel even more that he was right: I was the one who seduced him; I was the one who made him a monster.

At the same time, it enraged me to see how he kissed my mom, played with my sister and even joked around with me as if nothing had happened. But I believed I was making a sacrifice for my idea of a perfect family, and as long as the family was happy I could deal with it.

Eventually he started touching me. One night, he came to my bedside to kiss me goodnight and his tongue clawed its way down my throat. I tried pushing him away, but he held firmly to my wrists. A lifetime later he let go, withdrew his tongue and tucked me in.

"Good night, Sweetie...I'm sorry," he whispered hoarsely into my ear.

I rolled over to my side and cried the entire night. It would have been easier to hate him if he had been a total monster, but a part of me still loved him because he did things a normal father would do, like tuck me in and wish me goodnight.

fter that, he started touching me and rubbing against me with his clothes on whenever he got the chance. He even gave Vicky cold medicine to make her go to sleep after he picked her up from school so that he could be free to torment me. The abuse continued for a year.

Instead of speaking out, I turned goth. I painted my nails black, wrote suicidal poems, listened religiously to metal and alternative punk, and lost all faith in everyone, including myself. I knew my behavior was going to get attention, and I wanted my stepfather to notice. I wanted him to see the pain he was causing.

My obnoxious, hard-core music was also my defense mechanism, because it kept my stepfather away. When I blasted songs about hate and sorrow, his face would tighten and he would walk away from me. He knew why I was acting all emo and I believed he was even afraid of me.

My mom, on the other hand, had no clue why I'd changed so suddenly, and she began to worry. Once, when she demanded to know what was wrong, I almost told her. But then my stepdad called out from the living room asking what was for dinner, and I turned

I let the abuse continue because he made me feel like I deserved it.

away from her. My words would have put him on the street, and he didn't even have a job. Even though I hated what he was doing, I didn't want him to end up homeless. I also wanted to protect myself and my "perfect" family.

The abuse finally stopped when my stepfather found a job. I guess he stopped because we weren't home alone at the same time anymore. If he hadn't gotten a job, I think the abuse would have continued or even gotten worse.

I was relieved and hoped things would go back to normal. But I still felt depressed, and that's when I realized that everything I had been trying to protect by not telling anyone—my perfect family, my life the way it used to be—was ruined anyway. I couldn't stand to be next to my stepfather. My mother and I always argued because she didn't approve of my emo lifestyle and because I'd become distant from her. My perfect family was not so perfect, after all.

With this in mind, I finally felt it was time to let out my emotions. I told my two closest friends and afterward I cried with relief. But when they implored me to tell my mom, I refused. For a month they continued begging me, telling me he could do it again or even do it to my sister. I'd always had that fear for Vicky in the back of my mind, but when they said it aloud I felt the fear empower me and I finally mustered the courage to tell my mom.

It was a cool October evening, and I was walking silently with my mom toward my grandmother's house. I hadn't planned to tell her that day, but it was the first time we'd been alone together in awhile, and something told me it was time. I stopped walking and took a deep breath.

"Mom, I have to tell you something," I said.

"What is it?" My mom had a concerned look on her face that suggested she wasn't ready to hear what I was about to say, but it was too late to turn back.

"Mom, I don't know how to say this, and I've been wanting to tell you for a long time…" My voice began to falter and I started trembling and sobbing hysterically. "Mom, I'm sorry, but I didn't want to ruin your marriage. And Vicky, I couldn't have her grow up like me. And I was so afraid, and I felt ashamed and confused, but I still care for him…"

My words come out breathy and choked and my mom reached out to hold me steady. "What happened? Who hurt you? What are you talking about?" Her voice was high-pitched, and I could see the dread in her eyes.

"John molested me," I finally said, looking down at my dirty, black sneakers, wishing I could tap them like Dorothy and go back home, back to the old days where everything seemed perfect.

My mom began to cry, but then anger took control, and she firmly lifted my head and told me she was glad I told her. She asked me to tell her exactly what he'd done and for how long.

She'd had a similar experience with an uncle, and when she had tried to speak out nobody believed her. She believed my every single word, and I felt so relieved.

The next day my mom ordered Vicky and me to sleep over at my grandmother's house as she confronted my stepfather alone. I was forced to tell the rest of my family what happened after my mom called saying that my stepfather had tried to kill himself by overdosing on prescription pills.

When I heard that, I felt extremely guilty and regretted speaking out. I also felt ashamed to have to tell my family what had happened. I thought they would blame me for not speaking out sooner. But, like my mom, they believed me, and I was relieved.

My stepfather was sent to a psychiatric ward and then a facility for suicidal patients. When he returned a few weeks later, my mom, Vicky, and I had already moved into my grandmother's house. I begged my family not to call the police. I just wanted it to be over. But then my stepfather's sister told our pastor what had happened and he insisted on calling the police. After having to repeat my story almost 20 times to social workers, police officers, psychologists, and doctors until around midnight, I was assigned to a district attorney.

It was a good thing I found the courage speak up, because nobody else would have done it for me.

The story soon felt fake; I repeated it so many times that it became mechanical and I could tell it indifferently: "From about August of 2005 to July of 2006 my stepfather masturbated in front of me, touched and rubbed my private areas through my clothes, and kissed me once. There was no penetration."

When my lawyer asked if we wanted to press charges against my stepfather, I said no because I didn't want him to go to jail. Everybody talked about him as if he was some kind of monster without feelings. But I remembered coming home to him as a kid and giving him a huge bear hug. I remembered family nights when we all watched movies together. I couldn't understand why he had to throw away all those happy memories by molesting me, but I still didn't want him to end up in jail.

He didn't go to jail, but the abuse was put on his permanent record, and he was forced to go to therapy. I also got a restraining order on him until I turn 21, and he was no longer allowed to see Vicky unsupervised.

I was firmly advised to attend therapy myself, but I quit after two sessions. I just wanted to forget it had happened.

My family supported me and constantly reminded me that I had done the right thing by speaking out. And after I spoke out, my stepfather's sister and niece confessed that he had molested them as well. It made me feel proud to have been the one with the courage to speak out.

But for nearly two years, I wondered if I had made the right decision. My mom was depressed and my sister cried for her father at night. She didn't know why her parents had separated. The very thing I had tried to prevent by not speaking out had come true; my family was torn apart and my stepfather was practically homeless.

A few months ago, I decided to go back to therapy. I knew I wasn't healed and I finally felt ready to talk about what happened.

I see my social worker regularly, and she's helping me realize that I did make the right choice. She has reminded me of his other victims and that if I hadn't said something, he could have raped me or done something to my sister.

Recently, I learned that my mom and my family had suspicions about the abuse but stayed silent because they wanted to protect their own idea of a happy family. They didn't want to believe it could be true. Learning this made me realize it was a good thing I found the courage speak up, because nobody else would have done it for me.

Writing this story has also helped me feel better about my decision. I was so preoccupied with protecting other people, including my stepfather, that I failed to protect myself. I never let myself think about how I felt. Writing this has forced me to remember exactly what happened and how I felt.

My stepfather had no right to do what he did. I see that now. If anyone ever hurts me or makes me feel uncomfortable again, I will speak up right away. No man will ever make me feel like my stepfather did. Silence will never again be an option.

The author was 15 when she wrote this story.

Missing His Harmful, Hurting Hands

By Anonymous

One hot summer day I was on my way to a parade. When I saw my dad, I wanted to run. He was like a shadow hanging over me. He wrapped his arms around me like he missed me. Then I wanted to hug him, but being close to him made me afraid of what came next. He kissed me and held me so close. I did nothing.

I always want my dad to hold me close, to tell me that he misses me and loves me. But with my dad, it never stops there.

I pushed away and held on closer at the same time. I didn't want the closeness to stop but I didn't want it to go further. My arms burned from his hands because he gripped me too tight. He leaned me against the wall, put his hands under my shirt.

I felt violated. I wished I had died long ago. I wished that he would stop, but he moved on, telling me that he missed me and that I shouldn't forget him, because when I turn around he'll still be there. I cried—that was a first—but he didn't seem to notice.

I noticed, but I wished I would stop crying. I didn't want to feel anything or notice anything.

I felt violated by the eyes of people who didn't notice what was going on. Where was everybody? We were in a park, hiding behind the trees and the wall, in a shadow. From a distance it looked like we were girlfriend and boyfriend. All I could picture was nobody around, nobody wondering, "What is he doing to that girl?" Then I was one of them, not looking. I was in the third person. When I am in the third person, I watch a girl get hurt and it isn't me

When I was little, my dad was the guy who had all the candy I wanted. We were close. We would play games and talk about our business selling fruit. He was the best dad.

Then, when I was 8, our apartment burned down and my family moved into a shelter. My dad left us because he didn't want to stay with my mom. He left us alone with a mother who had no understanding of how to treat her kids. Her sadness left her for dead. She took her pills and went to sleep, and we knew better than to wake her up. She would hit my siblings and me for anything. It was like living with a monster.

He came back into my family's life after two years. He was very happy and said that he missed us. While my mom went out with her boyfriends and used drugs, he was kind, sweet, and stayed home with us (although he used crack, too). I forgave him for leaving us.

But one day when I was 9, I was in my room in the shelter when my father came in and closed the door. He sat on my bed and put his hand out. Everything got worse. When he started touching me, I didn't want him to know me. I had no feeling, everything felt out of order. He told me to keep it a secret, to pretend that it didn't happen.

After he left I crawled to the corner of my room and just sat there, trying to realize what had happened. My body felt like it was split into two people. One person felt good, the other felt bad. Emotionally I felt like nothing.

After that, he would come to me at night. In the day there was the passing touch that let me know what to expect. When he showed up, I felt like I was tied to the bed and I could not move. If I tried to resist, he hit me or held me down.

Later on, my dad wasn't making enough money to meet his drug habit, so I had to have sex with other guys. He'd be there and, after it was over, he'd carry me home. I loved his arms. After a while I fell in love with him and when he'd join the guys and me, I'd do whatever they wanted me to. I'd close my eyes and imagine that my dad was the only guy making love to me.

I always want my dad to hold me close, to tell me that he misses me and loves me. But with my dad, it never stops there.

I hated what he was doing to me, but I also loved my dad. He treated me like I was pretty. He made me feel good about my glasses, my shyness, and my imagination. He treated me like I was his wife and I loved that.

To keep from hating him, I blamed myself. I told myself that I led him on by wearing sexy clothes and that I could've stopped it if I'd wanted to. I believed he chose me because I was weak—I never even opened my mouth to scream. But in truth, rejecting him was not an option.

I wanted to tell my mom but she was always drunk or high or in her own world. Anyway, it seemed like she already knew. Sometimes she would call me a little slut, or tell me that if anything was happening I should tell her. I wanted to tell her because I wanted her to give me a hug. But that wouldn't have happened.

Instead, my mom and I would drink together. Then it felt like my mom cared. Once she bought me my own big bottle. Often, when I was just 10 years old, I would show up at school already drunk.

When my mom and I drank together we bonded in the way most drinkers do, by saying, "Cheers!" and drinking 'til the bottle was empty and there was nothing left between us but air.

I also remembered what my mom did when she was in pain. She cut herself in the bathroom and I saw the blood come down her arm. The first time I tried it, I wanted to die. I thought that would be better than letting my dad hurt me. But I found that just cutting myself was a relief. I do it to this day. It feels good. It feels like I am powerful and in control.

What really helped me, though, was that I learned to space out, to do what my dad said—pretend it didn't happen. I spent so much time outside of my body, outside of reality, that I began to have trouble telling what was real. When I was in pain, I would watch myself from far away, and then I didn't feel the pain. The opposite happened, too. Even now, I remember times from the past so strongly that I don't realize I'm in school or safe in my group home.

I hated what he was doing to me, but I also loved my dad. To keep from hating him, I blamed myself.

I was scared about what was happening to me, but I didn't know who to tell or if anyone would believe me. Then one day I was talking to my sister and we started making jokes. My sister said stuff like, "He's a poor choice of a man" and "He's a bitch." I said that he knew what to do to keep us quiet. Finally, she told me that my dad touched her. I told her that he did it to me also.

Telling each other what was happening felt like a break-through, but when I had to admit that it was real I wanted to go nuts and cry or scream.

I thought I'd feel relief after talking to my sister, but I just got sadder. I realized that everything that I'd been trying to pretend was OK actually felt wrong. And I realized that even though I'd told, I still couldn't face the truth. My sister could talk with the plainest face about what my dad was doing, but I only wanted to make jokes or to cry. I couldn't handle my emotions. Talking made it too real. I lost reality in a thick blanket of lies, protecting me from a touch that makes me want to jump and scream.

I got pregnant when I was 13. I went to the clinic alone. The door was so light, it felt like it wanted to let me go in with ease. Inside was the pine smell of freshly mopped floor.

The nurse called my name. When I tried to get up, I was stuck and I couldn't get out. The nurse led me to a room with one of those white tables with stirrups. The doctor sat there, just looking, touching his robe, smoothing out the wrinkles. I got undressed. The gown felt so crispy. I leaned back on the bed.

The nurse held my hand. "Relax, take a deep breath." The gas made me drowsy and I pretended that the nurse was my dad, watching me. When I woke up, my body was stiff. The smell of pine made me feel nauseous. A lady doctor stood over me. I didn't know whether to cry or smile.

"Who's the father?" she asked. My body froze. All I could think about was my opportunity to end this abuse, but I was afraid to end it. And truth was, I didn't know: Was it my dad or one of his friends?

When I was 14, my siblings and I all went into foster care. A year later, my sister and I went to court. The room smelled like wood and old paper. My lawyer took me to my seat and as I looked up, all I saw was lawyers.

I was so angry. I pretended my true self was throwing paper around the room. I was so upset, but I couldn't get the tears out. We both told what happened and they believed us. After that we got an order of protection against my dad. I thought that would keep him away but it didn't work.

It started again when I walked out of my school, outside my group home. I'd walk outside and there he was, ready to steal my body.

When I go out and run into him, I become deaf and mute. I hate the train station, I hate the quiet streets, I hate that my father comes to me so gently that you would think we're meeting for the first time. I can't say why I don't scream, why running is no option, why I'm frozen. I think I freeze because I want to pretend it's a dream and that when I wake up, it won't have happened.

I tell myself that if he doesn't hurt me, he'll hurt another girl or he'll hurt my sister. But that's just another lie to justify not screaming. What I can't face is that I'm not sure I want to stop it. I've already lost my mother, my oldest sister, and my two brothers. I don't want to lose my dad, too. I don't want to let go of my dream that he'll love me enough to stop.

So I pretend my father is my lover to protect myself from what my mind doesn't want to accept—that I'm getting hurt all over again, and that I'm not protecting myself but protecting him.

I've already lost most of my family. I don't want to lose my dad, too.

I love to sit alone in the park. My problem is that I know my dad will be there. Once he came and just stood next to me, looking at the water. I loved that. But usually when he shows up, I disappear. It happened a couple months ago. The rain dropped on me and I drifted away from my body.

"I can't believe we ran into each other," he said. I didn't know if I should hug him or kiss him, so I did nothing.

"I'm about to get some coffee. Do you want to come?" he said.

I pretended I wasn't the one going along. "Can you believe that girl?" I said to myself. "Going to a coffee shop with that man?" I got a coffee with sugar and milk. It tasted good.

"How are you?" he said when we sat down. The conversation was about school and my brothers, who are living at home again, without me. His hand rested on my leg. I held his hand and sipped my coffee.

"I'll play with you if you play with me," he said. I was so far away now. I looked at myself from a distance—a girl in a coffee shop, staring at her coffee.

"You remember how it goes." It made me sick. I wished I had something to stab him with, or that I could wake myself from my dream. Then my dad said something strange. He told me he was moving away. I didn't know how to feel. It was like saying goodbye to my first crush.

"I love you," he said.

"We'll keep in contact," I said, but I didn't ask where he was moving and he didn't tell me. I gave him a hug, a kiss, and he was gone like the wind.

Since then I haven't seen him. I heard from my mother that he did move out and I don't know where he's gone. It scares me not to see him. It feels like I'm losing that part of me that had someone's full attention. I feel incomplete. I'm not sure if my father will be back. Right now, I don't feel any relief that he's gone. I feel only loss, like I'm missing one of my fingers.

I wonder, "What will I feel if I never see my dad? Will I feel better about myself? Will I go back to normal? Can I put it behind me?" I want to forget about everything that happened, but how can I let go of something that has been part of me for almost 10 years?

The truth is, I'm afraid to give up on his loving touch. I guess I've gotten addicted to it. His hands are like alcohol; they intoxicate me and I want more. I miss his harmful, hurting hands.

The author was 17 when she wrote this story.
She later graduated from high school and attended college.

Fernando Quinones

A Partner in His Crime?

By Anonymous

I was 4 when my mother, my sister, and I moved in with my grandmother. My grandmother and mother both worked, so my grandmother's friend in the building, Denise, watched my sister and me during the day. Denise had two daughters about our age, Christine, who was 5, and Sparkle, who was 3. I fit right in between the two girls' ages and I liked being around them. I figured that living with my grandmother was going to be the best experience yet.

As we four girls got older, we stayed close. We had secret picnics in the park and went bike riding around the block. I was having the time of my life.

Soon Denise's significant other, Johnny, started hanging around the apartment a lot too. He was a short guy with a wide nose. At first, I didn't really pay much attention to him. But when

I was 6, he moved in with Denise. Over the years he became a regular face. He was also one of the few older males I knew. My father was never really there much so I didn't have a male figure in my life. Johnny seemed as good an older male figure as any, so I liked having him around.

Then, when I turned 10, things started getting strange with Johnny. He liked to play hide and go seek with us girls. But every time I hid, Johnny always found me first. I thought it was because my hiding places were too easy to find, so I started hiding in cabinets and closets. But Johnny kept on finding me first. I thought that was strange. I thought, "He's cheating, my hiding places are better than Christine and Sparkle's." But I also felt happy, because I was getting attention from him.

Then we switched games. We began play fighting. Johnny kept picking me to be on his team. I thought that was a real privilege. Being picked by him, an adult, made me feel better and larger than Christine and Sparkle. It made me feel important, like I was Cleopatra.

But when we played, it felt mostly confusing. Every time one of the girls would swing, Johnny would pull me in front of him and something hard would be touching my backside. I thought that it was one of his pants buttons. Except it kept happening. I started to feel as if he was making his buttons touch me on purpose, and that made me feel uncertain, so I stopped being on Johnny's team. I didn't pay any mind to it again until months later when he started acting even stranger.

One summer day I was playing with Christine and Sparkle outside, and ran into their home to use the bathroom. When I came out, Johnny grabbed me and spun me over to the other side of the wall. At first I thought he was going to hit me, because he had this glare in his eye. Instead he rubbed my cheek, then kissed it.

I smiled and tried to walk away. But Johnny held me there. He put his tongue in my mouth. He started rubbing my backside and kissing my neck. I suddenly felt as if he was doing something really bad. I began to cry. He told me not to cry because he was doing this out of love. He told me not to tell anyone because they would get jealous and hate me.

After he finally let me go, the only thing that ran through my mind was that I was going to be hated if I told anyone about what he did. That night, I wanted to ask my mother if a man should kiss me out of love, but I didn't ask her because I was scared she would hit me for it. I remembered the time when I was much younger and my mother hit me because I asked her if a boy should hold my hand. So I kept silent, even though it was burning me up inside.

Days later, I was watching TV at Denise's house while braiding my sister's hair when Johnny came in the room. Johnny acted as if he was going to change the channel, but instead he started poking me. I thought he was poking me to see a show, but when I turned around I saw he had pulled his penis out of his pants. He was trying to get me to touch it.

Johnny liked to play hide and go seek with us girls. But every time I hid, he always found me first.

I turned away and continued doing my sister's hair. Johnny reached for my hand. I pulled it away. I told my sister to move to another part of the room. She did what she was told, and I resumed braiding her hair. I didn't know why this was happening, but I no longer thought Johnny was a great role model. I decided he was disgusting.

I felt that every time I went to Denise's house there was going to be a problem with Johnny. Although no one else seemed to notice, it was now clear as day that everything he wanted to do to me was peculiar. In the beginning, when Johnny was choosing me for games, I had felt like I was the special one that Johnny loved and cared for. Now I was hoping that someone else would take my place.

Later, Johnny whispered that he was sorry and he would never do it again. I thought, "Yes! I won!" All I had to do was resist really hard and he would stop. Little did I know that I had won the battle, but he was going to win the war.

One night, Denise and Johnny had a few friends over and they were playing cards and drinking heavily. I was supposed to sleep at their house because my grandmother and mother weren't home. Before us kids went to sleep, Johnny came into the bedroom and saw where everyone was lying down. Much later, I woke up to the feel of the covers being pulled off me. Then I felt someone's hand going up my shirt. When I opened my eyes, I saw the hand was Johnny's. He put his hand over my mouth. He told me that he had to be my first in order for me to be a grown person. Then he said that I was not to tell anyone.

I didn't go back to sleep that night. I was afraid that if I did, he would come back and I wouldn't be able to stop him. I was also afraid that I would make him mad by trying to refuse him, and he would hurt me. I hoped that he would get someone else to love and care for, if this really was love. That way, no one would hate me and the touching would stop.

I began to spend less time at Denise's house. The nights my mother made me sleep over, I would lie awake and hope that Johnny was asleep. It never worked. He would come in and feel me up until he was satisfied.

Since I didn't think I could do anything to stop what was going on, I would lie there and pretend that I was asleep until he was done.

Over the three years that he molested me, I became used to just lying there and not saying anything. Even though I knew that something was wrong, I felt that if I told my mother, she would say that I was lying or she would blame me. I thought my grandmother would be furious at me because she told me not to play with grown men. I didn't need the burden of their anger as well, so I let it continue.

But this "love and care" that Johnny was giving me was making me a wreck. I would go to school in the morning, and before I got in the door I would chant, "It did not happen. It did not happen." If I did not say that sentence 20 times, I would think about what Johnny was doing to me all day. Repeating that sentence helped minimize the horrible thoughts.

Still, even when I said the sentences, I would sometimes have to excuse myself from class and go to the bathroom, where I would break down and cry. I was also beginning to get very hostile with teachers. The teachers would pat me on my back and tell me "Good job," and I would burst out with, "Don't touch me!" Boys would slap me on my butt and I would get a flashback of play fighting with Johnny, then I'd break down and cry.

I was feeling alone and violated by everyone around me. I thought I would be able to forget what happened if I no longer spent the night at Denise's house. But that was a dream that would only last a minute.

It didn't occur to me that I was the child and Johnny was the adult and that adults are supposed to protect kids, not hurt them.

The night of my mother's birthday, I was scheduled to spend the night at Denise's. I figured the usual would happen with Johnny and then I would go home and forget it.

That night, Johnny came in the bedroom before bedtime and checked where everyone was sleeping. No one paid any mind to it but me. Later I woke up to my spandex being almost completely removed. I was very afraid because Johnny had never gone this far. I tried to keep my legs closed tight. I tried to turn away, but he kept me on my back.

He was pushing himself into me when footsteps came down the hall. He quickly got off me and jumped into his pants. Denise came out of the shadows and into the room. She asked him what he was doing and he said he was checking on his son. She accepted his lame answer and went into the bathroom. In the morning, I was very sore and in pain.

I told my mother that I no longer wanted to stay at Denise's house. She asked why, and I lied. I said that Christine acted funny towards me when I spent the night. My mother gave me that "oh well" look, and then resumed whatever she was doing. She wasn't going to take a complaint about my oldest friend too seriously.

By the end of the school year, I had managed to almost completely avoid spending the night at Denise's house. But even though I rarely saw Johnny now, I still felt as if he were right there, wherever I was.

I started talking in my sleep. That made me scared that I would talk about what was happening with Johnny out loud and my mother would hear and go insane with anger. So I started waiting for my mother to be in a deep sleep before I closed my eyes.

What Johnny had done was now consuming me. I started regretting everything about my innocence. Why had I been flattered by his attention in the beginning? Why hadn't I realized that the way he always picked me on his team was strange? I started blaming myself for everything that had happened. I couldn't imagine how anyone would find Johnny to blame. It was my fault. I was the one who wore shorts and spandex over to Denise's house. Maybe if I had worn loose pants he would never have touched me.

It didn't occur to me that I was the child and Johnny was the adult and that adults are supposed to protect kids, not hurt them. It didn't occur to me that what Johnny was doing was dead wrong and that he was manipulating me by telling me that it was an act of love. It didn't occur to me that he could be put in jail for it. Instead, I felt bad that I had caused everything to happen. I thought that maybe I should apologize to Johnny.

I began to sink into something that is now known to me as depression. I didn't enjoy the things I used to enjoy. I blamed myself for anything that went wrong in my life. I still believed that if I told anyone about what Johnny did to me, I would be hated, but I also knew that keeping it inside was making it hard for me to live.

I began junior high school with a whole new attitude. A bad attitude. My temper stank and I went through so many mood swings. Eventually, a guidance counselor noticed what was going on with me.

The guidance counselor's name was Michele and she taught sex education. Her class was something that I did not want to be in. It made me feel really dirty. In that class I felt as if my body was filled with dirt patches. Every time we spoke about vaginas and penises, all I could think about was Johnny pushing himself on me. I thought that she was always directing that part of the class towards me, because she was always looking at me.

I vowed not to talk to her about Johnny, but I also hoped that she might figure it out if I gave her enough clues.

One day after class, Michele brought me to her office. When she began to talk, the phone rang. She answered it and I ran to the bathroom and threw up. For some reason, vomiting felt good. Michele came in the bathroom and asked what was making me so sick. I walked away without saying anything and went back to my next class.

After that, Michele kept being friendly with me. She always said hello to me in the halls. I didn't understand why she was still trying to speak to me, but it was nice to get the attention.

I started to think that I should try again with Michele, because she seemed like someone that I could talk to better than my mother. I vowed not to talk to her about Johnny, but I also hoped that she might figure it out if I gave her enough clues.

I started going to Michele's office nearly every day. We spoke about boys and men. She would answer my questions about sex. Soon I was feeling a strong bond with her. She was almost like an older sister.

One night during this time, my mother had to go out so she

made plans for us to spend the night at Denise's house. I objected again and again. I said that Christine and I were in a big fight, but my mother wouldn't budge. I had to sleep there.

As always, Johnny checked to see where I was sleeping. Then I came up with an idea of how to trick him. When the lights went out, I told Christine that my bed was too hard for my back, and we switched beds.

I woke up to the lights being turned on. It was Johnny. He had figured out that I was in a different bed and was looking for me, his victim. Eventually he turned the lights back off and left the room.

Later he returned with his breath full of liquor. I turned my whole body to the wall. He started prying the covers away from me. I started crying softly. I grabbed the covers and placed them back on top of me. He pulled them back and got on top of me.

Christine woke up and started to walk towards the bathroom. She didn't seem to notice Johnny, or at least she was pretending not to, because she was rubbing her eyes and walking in the opposite direction. Johnny crept off me and towards his bedroom. He had been so determined this time, and I knew that the next time I spent the night at Denise's, I might not be so lucky.

After that, I had Johnny on my mind every day and every night. He was like a virus that infected my brain and erased good stored data. I couldn't think about anything else. When I did my homework, I'd have another sheet of paper on which I'd write over and over again: "It did not happen." That sentence helped me feel sane.

But other times, I felt as if I were dying. My whole body felt paralyzed when Johnny came into sight. My soul was crying out for me to tell Michele, my guidance counselor, but the fear I had in my heart prevented me from telling. I tried to go to God for strength, but then I began to doubt that He would ever help me, because Johnny's touching me had been my fault. At least that's what I believed. Most of the time I hated myself rather than

Johnny.

The pain in my heart was eating away at the things that I felt for other people. I could no longer feel love from anyone. Not my parents or my grandparents. Because Johnny said what he was doing was love, I now thought of love as a curse that could only bring suffering.

Any thought of sexual feelings brought me down to ground zero. I no longer hoped for marriage one day and I stopped wanting kids. I didn't want love from anyone. Love usually involved someone touching me to hug me, and I no longer liked to be touched. I wanted to lie down and die just so I would stop hurting so much. I believed that I could die and I was not afraid to try.

If one person doesn't believe you, tell someone else. Keep telling until someone listens.

During one of my sessions with Michele, I had a quick flashback of Johnny's hands on my body. Feelings of failure and pain began to come back. Michele asked me how I thought of life and I told her that I wanted to die. I told her that I had a lot of pain in my heart and that I was tired of it. She kept me there in her office for over an hour. I thought that she was just in the talking mood.

When I got home that afternoon, my mother had this pissed off look on her face. She said she'd received a call from Michele. My mother told me that I had no pain in my heart and that I was only trying to get attention. That comment made my heart feel that much heavier. It was as if nothing in my world mattered to my mother. After my mother yelled at me, I went into my room, cried a little, and went to sleep.

By the end of the first semester I stopped going outside and began to keep to myself. I did not want any attention and I did not want to be seen. I began to keep a journal of plans of how to die. These plans gave me a sense of relief. I could go any second I wanted because I was well prepared. And I wanted to die.

The pain was crushing me. It felt like billions of thorns poking me at the same time. This feeling went on until I could not compose myself any longer and I knew I had to tell someone. Someone like my guidance counselor.

Towards the end of the school year, I told my guidance counselor that I had a friend who was being sexually abused and I needed her to help my friend. My counselor insisted that I bring my friend into her office, but the problem was that there was no friend. I told my Spanish teacher that I had lied to the guidance counselor about a story that was actually about me. I told her to tell my guidance counselor.

When I went to my guidance counselor the next day, she asked me to explain what happened to my friend. I did, and then she explained that my Spanish teacher told her that it was really about me and that she had to tell my mother. That just killed me right there. I could not tell my mother because she would blame me. I already thought that I was to blame and I did not need any extra help.

My mother was eventually notified and it was nothing but pure hell in my house. Like I thought would happen, she accused not Johnny, but me. She accused me of liking what Johnny was doing, and said that was why I continued to go over there.

Although I knew that I was going to be blamed, I had no idea that it was going to hurt like it did. But even though for a while the pain was worse, I soon found out that just telling people about it had somehow taken some of my pain away.

In April, I went to Mt. Sinai hospital for counseling. At first it was very hard for me to talk about the sexual abuse. It was opening up doors to things that really hurt on the inside. I hated those open doors. But talking about what Johnny was doing also felt like a weight was being lifted off my shoulders.

My therapist notified my mother again, to let her know that Johnny was still trying to molest me. Again my mother said that what Johnny was doing to me was my fault and I was only looking for attention. My therapist called the foster care system and filed a neglect case on my mother.

The system sent me to live with my father. While I was with him, we never really spoke about the abuse, but I could tell he was silently on my mother's side. He would say things to me like, "You did a very bad thing to the family." My therapist and guidance counselor told me that the abuse wasn't my fault, but hearing things like that from my father and mother made me wonder who to believe.

Still, it was a relief to not be near Johnny. By the time I entered the 9th grade I was feeling much better about myself. I had thrown away the book of death plans and I was living my life.

Eventually, in late October, I went into foster care. I was placed with an intelligent woman named Reana. She was very nice to me and she didn't like the fact that my mother did not believe me about the abuse. That made me feel that my mother, not me, was the one doing something wrong.

Now I am living comfortably with my foster mother. She listens to everything that I say and she loves me just like family. I guess that was all I needed in the first place. A new and improved heart.

I am no longer in contact with my parents because they are still holding grudges against me ever since I told my deepest secret. I still care for my parents, but I don't see how we can have a relationship right now. It would be too hard when they still blame me for the abuse.

Maybe the biggest thing that's happened is that I have decided not to blame myself for what happened with Johnny. The help that I received from my guidance counselor and my foster mother helped me to realize that it was not my fault. I am beginning to believe this is the truth in my heart as well as in my mind. I no longer have to say sentences to convince myself of anything.

The hardest part is thinking about what happened and accepting that it did happen. That still hurts and maybe always will. But it's easier to accept when I remember that it was not my fault. That makes me feel I have a little bit of control if anything like that ever happens again.

My little sister lives upstate with her father. I miss her so much. Denise's family still lives in their old apartment. I see them from time to time when I am visiting my friends, but we are not close anymore. There was never an investigation done about Johnny and I think he still lives with Denise. I would like to have the chance to confront Johnny without repercussions. I would tell him that I despised his "love" then and I despise it to this day.

Although I still struggle with memories of Johnny, I try to look at the positive aspects of my life. I now think of love as something that has to be given in a good and respectful way. I define it as something that is shared and makes people happy. Love is shared, but abuse is stealing your heart and playing with your head.

If anyone reading this is going through what I went through, please take my advice: no matter how bad or good the rapport is between you and your family members, do not wait until the abuse destroys you to tell someone. You have to tell when what's happening is hurting you. If one person doesn't believe you, tell someone else. Keep telling until someone listens. I know it's painful to tell, but what you're living with is far worse.

The author was 15 when she wrote this story.
She went on to graduate from high school and go to college.

Rudá Tillett

Facing the Truth

By Rosita Pagan

January 16, 1998 was a cold night. I was in my living room talking with my teenage daughter, Lyzette, when Alicia, who was 5, came out of her bedroom and told me, "Mommy, I'm tired."

"OK, go to bed, sweetie," I said.

"No, Mommy," she said, "I'm tired of being Daddy's wife."

That instant I felt numb, shocked. I couldn't believe what I was hearing.

Alicia repeated herself and I started to cry. Lyzette, her face full of tears, said, "I was afraid that someday he would try something with her."

Lyzette and I had been through this before, when Alicia was just 3 months old. Lyzette had come to me and told me that my husband had gone into her room and felt her legs up while I slept. That day, I told him that he had two choices—he could walk out the door, or fly out the window.

I believed Alicia's father had targeted Lyzette because she was not his daughter, so I didn't think he was a threat to Alicia, his biological child. Still, I wouldn't let Alicia's father see her. He went to court and filed a petition for custody. I told my lawyer what Alicia's father had done to Lyzette, but he didn't bring it up, and I didn't tell the judge myself because I didn't want to start a huge fight in court. I feared that might hurt my case. The judge ordered me to allow Alicia to visit him on weekends.

When Alicia confronted me with the truth, I wished I'd told the judge what had happened to Lyzette. I felt so conflicted and guilty. I didn't know what to do to help my daughters so I just hugged them both. It wouldn't ease the pain but I wanted to let them know that I'd always be there for them.

I hadn't been able to protect my children, and I couldn't help them to recover, so what good was I?

That night, I couldn't sleep. All that ran through my mind was, "How could he?" I felt worthless as a mother. I believed I should have seen the signs, especially because my uncle raped me when I was about 6 years old. (I didn't know then that people who've been abused themselves often don't recognize the signs of abuse in their children.)

The pain I felt being raped as a child came back to me when I thought about what my daughter had been through. I knew I didn't want to respond the way my mother did—she didn't believe me. Being raped haunted me for a long time.

I had thought the distrust and fear that I'd felt from being raped was behind me. But my fears came back when Alicia told me she was molested. I thought, "Is this ever going to end? Will it just go on from generation to generation?"

Although I felt despair that night, I knew that I had to do whatever Alicia and Lyzette needed me to do to help them heal. I wouldn't do what my mother did. I was determined to stop that cycle.

After Alicia told me she'd been abused, I noticed that she began to act strangely. When she was playing alone, she would lay down her stuffed animals, get on top of them and start humping them like a man would make love to a woman. That freaked me out. I didn't know then that it is common for girls who've been sexually abused to "act out" like that.

Alicia also started to touch herself. One night when she was in the bath, I noticed that she was very quiet. I went to check up on her and saw her touching her private area. I screamed and she got scared.

"What are you doing?" I said. I didn't mean to embarrass her, but I couldn't believe that a 5 year old was capable of masturbating.

Alicia told me, "What the lady does on TV." I wondered, "Was he having her watch porn?" I felt that if Alicia's father was present I would have strangled him with my bare hands.

After I finished bathing her, I got a knot in my throat and an eerie feeling. I sat in the living room, thinking, "Why is this happening? Why does she have to go through this?" I started crying.

I decided I needed a beer, so I took one and then another. That night I must have drunk six or eight beers. I felt good for the first time in months. The beer made me forget feeling down.

The next day when Alicia came home from school, I drank while watching her. As the months passed my drinking got heavier and heavier, to the point that I couldn't function without having a beer first. I began to think it didn't matter if I was drunk or sober. I hadn't been able to protect my children, and I couldn't help them to recover, so what good was I?

About a year later, the foster care system took my children from me.

It's a long story what happened when my children got taken away. The nightmare of sexual abuse had turned into a worse nightmare—the nightmare of being absolutely unable to protect my kids.

Finally I was sent to detox and to rehab upstate. Once I'd been sober for a month or so, I started feeling better about myself and began to believe I could get my life back on track. I told myself, "I have to get my family back. I'm not worthless. I can accomplish things if I make an effort."

The first foster mother had the girls for one year, but during that time, no one told her that Alicia had been sexually abused. The foster mother couldn't handle Alicia's sexual acting out. She was a religious person and she couldn't believe that a little girl would act that way. The caseworker took Alicia to therapy, but she didn't tell the therapist about the abuse, either. The doctor diagnosed Alicia with Attention Deficit Disorder (ADD) and treated her for that.

When my children moved to a second foster home, the mother understood the signs. She asked me, "Has Alicia ever been molested?"

"Yes," I said. "Why are you asking me this question?"

"Because Alicia does some sexual things that are strange for a girl her age," she told me. But she didn't know how to handle her behavior, either. Whenever she saw Alicia touch-

I am proud of myself and my daughters. We broke the cycle of denial in my family.

ing herself, she would tell Alicia to stand in a corner for a long time.

Neither of the first two therapists that Alicia saw were able to help her at all, but I was sure someone could. Once my girls came home I went to the Northside Center in Harlem and explained to the intake person that Alicia was molested and had ADD. The social worker who did an evaluation told me Alicia didn't have ADD, she was just dealing with the trauma of being abused. Finally, she began to get the proper care.

Alicia was seen by a social worker, Susan, who took the time to earn Alicia's trust. That helped Alicia open up and speak about the abuse. Alicia felt comfortable with Susan. She looked forward to seeing her every Friday. She would tell me, "Mom, today I'm going to visit Susan and we are going to talk and play. I like Susan a lot."

At every session, Susan would give me a note explaining Alicia's progress, and twice a month we would meet as a family. In her notes, Susan would explain what she asked Alicia and how Alicia responded. Susan asked her, "Why do you feel you have to touch yourself?"

"Because sometimes it feels good."

"What if you don't touch yourself? How do you feel?"

"I feel bored."

One practical thing Susan suggested was that I keep Alicia occupied by asking her to do chores, reminding her to read a book, or giving her questions to answer. Susan also suggested that we could grow closer if I just made conversation with Alicia. I started to ask her, "Did you make any friends today? How was school? What did you eat for lunch?"

She also suggested that, because touching herself was something Alicia felt she had to do, I shouldn't leave her alone for long periods of time, including when she showered. Over time, she thought Alicia's impulse to touch herself would calm down and that she would be able to return to being a little girl. That way she could safely explore her sexuality once she got older.

Those eight months Alicia went to Northside helped her cope with her feelings. She stopped the sexual behaviors and she learned not to be afraid to talk to me, regardless of the topic. Now she even asks me questions about sex at times, and I explain the answers to her without feeling upset about the past.

Alicia's therapy helped me feel more at ease. The sexual abuse seemed to be having less of an impact on her day by day. It seemed like my whole family was finally beginning to recover.

Today, I feel like my family is not as marked by the abuse or by fear. I am proud of myself and my daughters. We broke the cycle of denial in my family. I faced what my daughters went through, and I faced my own past, too.

My daughter needed therapy and I needed rehab to make me love myself again and help me deal with negative feelings like shame, betrayal and worthlessness. But I believe that today my daughters and I are better off because we didn't hide. We were strong enough to face the truth.

Rosita wrote this story for Rise, *a magazine by and for parents involved in the child welfare system. Reprinted with permission.*

Making It Out

By Anonymous

As a little child growing up in southwest Belize, in Central America, I was very happy, even though our family was really poor. My mother had five kids in the house. She struggled with us, clinging from one man to another, looking for care. I always felt safe, though. Every day I would wake up in the morning and go outside and play with my friends.

It was calm and breezy the day everything changed. I was 6 years old and went up to my neighbor's to play with his kids, like always.

I was waiting in the living room, playing with a little toy car, when the dad dragged me into his room, pulled down his pants, and said, "Now pleasure me." I was shocked, because I did not understand why he was doing this. His wife was right in the kitchen cooking, only a couple feet away.

When he was finished with me, I was put outside as if nothing ever happened. After that day, whenever I went up to play with his kids, he would sneak a touch between my legs or slide his hand under my shirt when no one was looking.

At 6 years old you don't know about sex and what is wrong or right. Every time he touched me I was confused and didn't understand what was happening, but I thought it was okay for him to do that.

Since I didn't know it was wrong, I never told anyone. Besides, I wasn't someone who spoke up for myself. I was the spitting image of my mother.

My mom was shy and quiet, and she was always in another world. She never left our house, not even for some fresh breeze when it was hot. She would stay in her small bed and watch TV all day, or just stare into space.

I felt I was only in the world for other people's satisfaction.

Still, I knew she loved me. When I had nightmares, she would let me climb into her bed and assure me that no ghost or monster would get me. Then she would sway me back to sleep right in her arms.

Today, I think my own shyness was a weakness that other people saw in me very strongly. When I started school, I would get jumped by my peers and go home with one or two missing teeth. People bullied me because I was weak. I would cry to my mother, but all she could do was wash my mouth out with salt water to stop the bleeding. I thought the sexual abuse was just another phase I had to go through, like being bullied.

About a year after my neighbor started molesting me, a friend of his raped me. This man was a regular presence in the yard where we always hung out. He came there to smoke weed and cause mischief. One day he was watching me and my friend play and joke around. As usual, we didn't pay him any attention.

I was on my way home when he came out of nowhere, put his arms around me, and rubbed my back, as if we were more than strangers.

I knew that this was not supposed to happen, so I tried to move away. But just like the first time with my neighbor, I was so frightened that he overpowered me. He pulled me into the trees so he could keep anyone from seeing what he was about to do to me.

In my mind I wanted so much help, but my body couldn't seem to find the strength to get up and walk to a precinct.

When he was finished, he had the damn nerve to say goodnight and ride off on his bike.

Afterwards, I couldn't understand why I just stood there while he eagerly unbuttoned my shirt and unzipped my pants, without trying to escape or fight back in any way.

I went home and said, "Mommy, I think I just got raped." She looked at me in a horrified way and laid me out on the bed, checking to see if the pervert had left any semen in me. She didn't see any and spanked me because she thought I was lying. Why had I worried her like that? I didn't mention it again because I felt bad that I scared her and made her worry. I thought I had just made things worse.

But I couldn't stop thinking about it because the man kept coming back to the yard as if nothing had happened. When I saw him, he would give me a smile, like he had just finished enjoying something. I would feel my blood crawl through me and I would quietly flee. My heart would just start pounding, and I'd feel as if a bomb would soon explode inside me.

One day my principal pulled me out of class for being absent and late a few times. Her office was pretty intimidating. I felt guilty when she asked me what was going on at home. Somehow, I told her what had happened and how I wasn't sure if that kind of thing was supposed to be happening to me. I started shivering because I thought I was in trouble. Even though being raped wasn't my fault, I felt as if I had just committed a crime.

My principal called social services. I was relieved that she believed me, but I still wasn't sure if what was happening to me was wrong. I didn't know if I wanted the men to get punished. All I knew was that I needed someone to talk to.

But instead of anything happening to those men, I was put in foster care. I was taken away from my family without even a chance to say goodbye. And instead of being safer, I only found more abuse. Looking back, it felt like that was the day I threw my life into the trashcan.

I moved in with an aunt, and I thought I was special because she wanted to take care of me. But in her eyes I was just a housemaid. I didn't get to see my brother and sisters, who were trapped back in the group home, and my aunt wouldn't let me see my mother, either. My aunt said she was "loco." After two years we moved to New York and I haven't seen them since.

I felt sad and zoned out in New York, and the only thing I could do was mope around. I think now that my vulnerability soon made me an easy target for my cousins and other men.

My cousin started sexually abusing me when I was about 7, not too long after they took me in, and kept on until I was 14. At first I didn't know how to react to all the rubbing up against me and sneak touching behind doors. But when it kept happening, I knew it was getting out of hand. I had to do something, fast.

"Auntie, I don't like what your son is doing to me," I remember saying one day. She asked what I meant and I explained, but Auntie insisted I didn't know what I was talking about.

"You're only 7, how do you know what sex is?" she said. "Shame on you. You shouldn't accuse people of things that aren't true. What did I tell you about lying to me? Get out of my face before I beat you."

I got that defeated, helpless feeling again, like when I told my mom back in Belize about being raped and she didn't believe me.

The blood in my body was crawling all through me.

I didn't know what to do anymore, so I let my cousin keep molesting me over and over again. There were times I told him to stop and that I was not comfortable with it. I thought that because he was family that I could reason with him and try to make him see what he was doing was wrong. But he never listened. Once he saw that his mom didn't see him as the pervert he was, he had the upper hand.

Then I tried to fight him off. Every night I would be up waiting. I knew if I was awake, I could be more focused on fighting him. But when I tried to resist, he would punch or choke me. I hated that I was weak and helpless. I wanted to not be so easy to handle, but I was.

It was like parachuting into the sky, when the detectives believed me over my cousin. I felt free.

When I would wake up in the morning with undried tears and new bruises, my cousin would tell his mom that I had provoked him. She'd believe him and shrug it off. There was nothing I could do about it. I didn't have the right to fight back.

One day I made the mistake of telling my cousin, "I'd rather be back home in foster care than here with you guys." He told my aunt what I said and she said, "Oh really? You want me to send your ass back to Belize? Because I could pack you up and send you on that plane right now without an ounce of pity."

Then she told me, "Your goddamn mother—you're ungrateful just like her. Did you know she had your brother at 15? Her father raped her and the woman didn't say a thing. She confessed when her belly started showing. You're going to be just like her, undependable and nothing."

I stood there without saying a thing. How could my mother be raped by her own father? But then, if my cousin had no conscience about raping me, I could see how that could happen. I shivered and stared at the floor without looking up. I wanted to die. I felt as if the whole house had just crumbled down on me without any warning. I thought, "When is this cycle of family incest going to stop?"

I felt I was only in the world for other people's satisfaction. I felt like I couldn't fight my cousin anymore and he was winning. My body was like sugar and my cousin couldn't get enough.

On TV, I would watch movies about rape and sexual abuse. I saw women who were brave and stood up for themselves. I realized that I couldn't be trapped all my life in this world where everything was wrong.

But going to an authority like the cops felt impossible. In my mind I wanted so much help, but my body couldn't seem to find the strength to get up and walk to a precinct. I felt like a million-ton weight was tied to my feet. I didn't know who to trust.

Finally my friends noticed my cuts and bruises and asked me what was happening. I was so desperate that I told them the truth. At first they were shocked. They didn't know how to react. I was scared about my aunt finding out, so I told them not to tell anyone.

But soon after that, my cousin Rachel's husband raped me when I was over their house. I was frozen, in shock that this was happening again with a different guy. Afterwards he threw me aside as if I was nothing. He warned me not to tell anyone about our "encounter" and left.

I freaked out. Was he going to keep coming back and make me his mistress? I wanted to cry, but something told me I must be strong and not to give up yet. I decided I should try telling my family about it. I didn't want to believe that they didn't care what happened to me. Maybe this time they would help.

When I told Rachel that her husband had raped me, she looked at me for a long time, turned around, and got my aunt. They stood in front of me with glaring eyes that could almost melt the skin off you.

"What are you trying to do? Ruin my marriage? You know what I think—you're the one who is coming on to him! You slut!"

They went on like that for about an hour, and then my aunt whipped me.

Two months later, my dean pulled me out of class. She said, "I've heard some disturbing things about you that I want to hear from your mouth, not others. Is there something you want to talk about?"

She told me that the day before, when I was absent, she had questioned my friends. They panicked and told her my secrets and all the things I was going through at home. I stood there in shock. I couldn't believe they had done that. "OK, don't panic," I thought.

The dean was one of my favorite teachers and I couldn't deny that she cared, so finally I told her everything. I told her about my uncle and the molestation I had to endure every night from my cousin. I spilled out about my aunt's criticism and abuse, and how I felt like an outsider. After I told her everything, I felt as if a whole ton of metal had been lifted from my shoulders.

My dean stayed quiet for a moment and then said, "I'm sorry you had to go through all that." Then she said she had to report this to someone. I knew that meant the cops, and I felt the hairs on the back of my neck stand up. I was terrified. But she assured me that everything was going to be OK and no one would harm me anymore.

At the precinct, they brought in my aunt and my cousin. My cousin tried to deny everything and my aunt pretended she didn't know what was going on. But the detectives had heard my story first and they believed me.

It was like parachuting into the sky, when the detectives believed me over my cousin. I felt free. For once I could hold my head up high and not be ashamed. I chose to be humble and reserved, but in my heart I couldn't stop smiling.

After that long, dreaded night, I was put into foster care and since then nothing has been the same. I am no longer being sexually abused and put down like a mangy dog.

It's only been about a year, but now that I'm in a safe place

I've been trying to recover and make sure it never happens again. It's not easy. Many nights I can't sleep. When my mind is not occupied, my past seems to jump out of nowhere to give me a kiss, and the things that have happened seem to spin all around me again, mockingly.

I try to keep my mind busy by reading or listening to music. I fish for adventures and hobbies so my head won't drift off to things in my past.

I'm in therapy, but I haven't felt ready to talk about what happened. I think I am still recovering from everything. I don't feel comfortable enough to spill my heart out there so easily. Talking about my past makes it seem so real and alive again. All the memories just keep flashing back, and, sadly, I can't handle it.

Since it's hard for me to talk about my past, maybe my writing can do the talking for me. I wrote this story because I want readers to understand where I'm coming from. I also wanted to show other victims like me that they should never give up on themselves, no matter how tough things may be.

I still feel vulnerable, but I am getting through it slowly. Even though I have been through the cycle of my mother's life and some of the things she went through, I am not like her. My mother couldn't find a way to escape. She gave up on herself and the world, never coming back.

When I think about my future, I get scared because I don't know what's in store for me. But at least now I can make my own choices, which is important. I don't stay in the house crunched up in a corner because I am afraid of men. I go out and explore the city. I travel and I am not afraid. I'm starting to take control of my life, and that helps me to feel stronger.

The author was 16 when she wrote this story. She earned her GED and was awarded a full scholarship to college.

Ruda Tillett

Painting My Way Through

By Anonymous

They say that a picture is worth a thousand words. I draw pictures. I was born an artist. I've used my drawings to open the window to my life, so I could let people know I was in danger, disappear into my fantasy world, and get my problems off my chest. I hoped that someone who saw my pictures could help me feel alive.

My sister taught me to draw when I was about 5 or 6 years old. My first picture was of mermaids jumping in and out of the water, a sunset that would never go down, and a rainbow that rained out Skittles of all assorted colors. They hit the water and lit up the page for days.

My godmother, who worked at my school, was the first to notice my artwork, which consisted of cats and little children running all over the place. She adored every picture I drew. She would hang them up in her office and tell all the teachers that my sister and I were going to become famous artists when we got older, and that she would buy our first pieces.

As I got older, my artwork became a way to dream. I never really had toys, so I drew a few and cut them out. I would play for hours at night. Then I would hang my toys on the walls around my bed and I would talk to them, and in my mind they would answer me back. At night I would dream about my sister and me flying away to a land on water where mermaids lived and where the Skittles fell from the sky.

But when I was about nine or ten my godmother got very disturbed when I gave her a picture of a girl tied to a bedpost being touched by someone. She asked me what the picture was about, and I never did tell her who the girl was—because she was me. My mother and father had started using drugs, and my father began raping me and forcing me to have sex with strangers. I was afraid to tell my godmother my secrets because my dad would get mad at me.

My godmother called my father. I don't know what they talked about, but I guess he convinced her that I was OK. That evening, my father called me at home. He was at work. "Be in my room when I get home!" he said. "OK," I told him. I already knew what would happen. I just wished it would be in my room so that I could go away with my friends, the toys on my wall.

Usually, when my dad came into the room and got on top of me, I would look up at the walls and think about my toys so I could drift away from my body and feel no pain. We would go all over the world and play games, fly through the sky.

But when my father got home that night, he climbed eagerly into the bed and said, "If you scream, it will only hurt more," and, "I want you to draw another picture of this and see what happens." I could hear his voice echoing in my head and throughout the room. I had to say goodbye to my dreams. When I came back from my journey, my father was still there and the pain was there. I couldn't drift away with the pain occupying my thoughts.

After that incident, I never wanted to draw in school again. But for the next few years I did anyway because I was afraid to draw at home. I drew pictures of dark rooms, men and money all over, or even blood and claws I imagined belonging to my father. He was a monster. Those pictures helped me express my feelings about the sexual abuse, the things my dad and his friends forced on me. The pictures were ways to let people inside of my home without speaking.

The pictures were ways to let people inside of my home without speaking.

My mother used to tell my sisters and me that if we ever got touched by anyone to tell her or write her a letter. So I left my drawings on the floor on purpose so that my mother would get a clue about what was going down. The pictures showed a girl in a room tied to a bed, crying, and a group of men counting money or sniffing cocaine.

I thought my mother might talk to me or even ask me why I was drawing such violent or scary pictures. But when I left signs for my mother to see, she would just yell at me, then show them to my dad and ask him if I was talking to him about any boy I was sleeping with, even though I was only about 11 years old.

A few years later, my sisters and I got brave enough to speak up. We talked together in our room.

"You know Mommy and Daddy are on drugs, right?"

"We need to tell them to stop cause we don't have no food and no money."

"What do we do?"

"We need to tell them how we feel right now."

Together we went to their room to tell our parents how we felt.

Our mother wasn't happy at all. I remember her words: "I don't have to stop for no damn kids." And, "If you like your older sister as your mother, then she can take you and you can go live with her."

Our father was cool. He said, "Let them speak!" And, "We'll stop, OK?" Then he started to wash the dishes and comfort our brothers, who were crying because of our mother's screaming.

I went into the other room and started drawing. My drawings were symbols of hope that someone could come and help my family someday, and remembrances of what I used to have in this once happy home. I remembered the laughs we shared, the fun we had, all of the things we did that seemed to have just washed away.

My mother came in and grabbed my drawings and ripped them up. I felt an emptiness in my heart. My heart felt like those little pieces of paper. When she tore them up, I felt my future would never bring happiness to me. At that moment I saw that I was stuck in her world. I feared I would grow up and be needy for a drug or a guy, like she was.

When my mother was finished, I picked up the pieces of my pictures and went to the park and buried them in the ground so that no one would ever see them again. I stayed in the park for about an hour, thinking that soon I would have to get rid of all my pictures because they were unsafe in my home.

But I could not stop drawing. My pictures were a part of me. I began to write and put my thoughts in a journal under my bed. I illustrated my journals with my drawings and soon I had a powerful log of my messed up home life.

I also began to draw on my body, on the many places that were violated by others. Those places felt like they belonged to other people. They felt so wide open that they cried out for a new feeling. I drew weapons to protect them. I wanted to own them, like I had owned my drawings on the walls.

So that I wouldn't go crazy, I started finding little places where I could hide from my dad. The closet was one good place. In one corner I put pictures of my cats, little girls who do nothing all day but play, and a monster being slaughtered by a blank face that doesn't want to see what its hand does.

I made sure that my dad and mom stayed out of the closet.

I couldn't put new pictures up around the bed, though, so I could never drift away with the toys on my walls. When my dad would come into my room, I would just take the damn pain and choke on it. Unable to drift away, I began to change inside. I become a very shy person. I was scared to open my mouth about anything.

Soon I began to notice that, though my life was an incomplete canvas, it seemed like I had no power to paint myself out of all of my troubles. I felt like I was letting my father win, letting my brush paint without any control over how the paint was flowing. I was painting lies just so I could survive. I didn't even recognize my own picture on that damn canvas.

My mother came in and grabbed my drawings and ripped them up. My heart felt like those little pieces of paper.

One rainy night I was inside my closet drawing pictures of princesses and pasting up pictures of places around the world that I wanted to go and see. My dad came into my room with a belt in his hand. The thunder started to roll as he took me by the shirt and started to yell at me, telling me that I could be broken if I refused him any longer.

That night, I told him that I was going to tell my godmother if he did not stop touching me. He slapped me in the face. With my mouth bloody, I looked out the window and tried to drift away as he touched me, talking into my ear.

I felt the raindrops from the window falling down on us and began to think that I wasn't the only one who could see what was going on. The rain and the outside world were watching.

As soon as the thunder stopped, I knew that it would not be too long before my father would be judged and get his fair share of the agony. It might not be that day or that week, but I was going to tell. I was going to make my escape from that hell and paint a picture of my life for the entire world to see. I would open up the colors of my rainbow and see to it that he got what he deserved.

Not much later, I did confide in teacher. I didn't use pictures—I wrote her poems, using figurative language like a code, then going into greater detail about what was happening to me. She told my godmother, and I got placed in care.

After that, I started writing a lot more than drawing. In my daily diary, I could write plainly about the many things happening in my life. I was ready to speak, to let it out to anyone who would listen to me. I didn't want to hide anymore or be scared. There was nothing and no one to be afraid of. I was free. My hell world and my fantasy worlds are behind me.

The author was 18 when she wrote this story.
She later went to college to study art therapy.

Freddy Bruce

Speaking Up

By Akeema Lottman

If you've suffered any form of abuse, it can be difficult to speak up, especially if the abuse is still going on. We wanted to find out more about how abuse can affect you, why it's so hard to report, and how you can begin to heal. I interviewed Shelly Petnov-Sherman, a social worker and therapist in Manhattan.

Q: What are the effects of abuse?

A: The first effect—and the most tragic—is the lack of trust. There's a sense that you're not safe and grownups aren't safe and the world isn't safe. People react to that feeling in different ways. Some people become aggressive and bully others or use drugs and alcohol to numb their feelings. Others try to be really, really nice to everybody so no one will hurt them. They don't set limits and boundaries with people, and sometimes they get walked on.

Both girls and boys sometimes lose respect for their bodies, which can be devastating because our bodies are the first place where we find our self-esteem. Many children who have been abused have a great difficulty having healthy adult relationships.

If the abuse continues for a long time, the victim may even start to identify with the abuser. It's a way to survive the trauma, but it can have very negative effects. The victim may take on some of the character traits of the abuser and think that he has the right to abuse others.

With all of these effects, the emotional impact can get worse the longer the abuse goes on, which is why it's so important to speak up and get help as soon as you can.

Q: What can make it hard to report abuse?

A: The thought of coming forward can be scary. It takes tremendous courage to report abuse, because often the abuser is threatening you with all sorts of horrible consequences if you don't keep the secret.

Also, you may have mixed feelings about turning against the abuser, especially if he or she is a family member or loved one. If this is the only attention you get, then this may be how love is defined and experienced by you. No one wants to give up love, no matter how harmful it may be.

When it comes to loved ones, we all have the ability to make different compartments inside of us. So, in one way we know that what the abuser is doing is wrong, but then there is another compartment where we may keep feelings like, "If I tell, he won't love me anymore and I will be totally alone." Or, "If I tell, I will be destroying my family and they will all blame me," and so on. The conflict between these feelings grows and becomes really confusing inside our heads.

Q: I've heard that kids often blame themselves when they're abused. Why is that?

A: Somewhere inside all of us we think we're in full control of what happens to us. So the victim may think he's done something that caused the abuse. That may be the only way he can make sense of what's happened to him.

Or the abuser may tell the victim that the abuse is her fault, and the victim has no trusted adult to talk to for help in sorting out what's true. The kid feels responsible, when in fact it has nothing to do with her. It's the responsibility of adults to keep children protected and safe.

If you're being abused, it's important to remember that you're not at fault.

Q: What are some common feelings kids have after reporting abuse?

A: Children and teens who have reported abuse often have a really wide range of feelings. There is often a sense of guilt because they have developed an emotional connection with the abuser and now think they've betrayed the abuser by telling. They might worry that they're responsible for the consequences that come to the abuser. They ask, "What will happen to them?" instead of "What has happened to me?" That guilt can be made worse in cases where families blame the victim for coming forward.

On the other hand, there can also be a sense of relief about reporting the abuse, especially if a child is responded to in a caring, respectful way. The way an adult responds when you tell them can have a really big effect on how you recover.

Q: How should an adult respond?

A: It's extremely important that the victim be believed and protected immediately. But sometimes there will be family members who don't believe you and accuse you of making it up. Or in some very disturbed households, it's sometimes ignored altogether.

The consequences of reporting abuse and not being believed can be, in my mind, more harmful to the victim than even the abuse itself. Not believing that a child has been abused sends a message that what has happened to the child is OK. No way is it ever OK. It can set you up for a pattern of abusive and destructive relationships for a lifetime if you don't receive help.

Q: When is the best time to speak up? Should you wait until you can show evidence of the abuse, like bruises?

A: Don't wait. Don't ever wait. The time to speak up about abuse is as soon as you can, the moment it happens, if possible. Or even before it happens. If you're afraid of someone, if you get that yucky, sick feeling in your stomach when you're around a person and feel creeped out by them, speak up. Find someone you trust—a teacher, counselor, the parent of a friend, a doctor— and keep telling until you find someone who takes you seriously. With any kind of abuse, kids often don't realize that their real source of power is to tell someone.

Q: What can you do to help yourself recover?

A: Get treatment, get therapy, for as long as you need it. Therapy can help you express this pain, to let it out. When it comes to abuse, secrets are poisonous. You've got to find someone you can share your secrets with who will believe you and validate your feelings.

Try to have people around you who love you, who believe you, and keep you safe. And as you go forward through life, surround yourself with good people. That can mean family, church, schools, or any other group of people that support you and make you feel good.

When you've been abused, your basic trust and connections to people have been damaged. Those bridges can be rebuilt by reaching out to a trusted teacher, social worker, therapist or other good people around you. Seek them out.

Akeema was in high school when she conducted this interview.

Patrick Liebert

Trying to Bury My Past

By Anonymous

After about a year of dating my boyfriend, Kevin, I began to have frightening flashbacks of the sexual abuse I experienced as a child. Since the flashbacks started, I've been uncomfortable having sex with Kevin. I've even started feeling threatened and victimized, the way I felt as a child, even though Kevin is not abusive toward me.

I never truly enjoyed sex, but after the flashbacks began I started to feel as if I wasn't even in the room anymore. I felt like a doll being rocked back and forth in a cradle while Kevin had sex with me. It reminded me of my father molesting me as a child.

I wanted to tell Kevin, or stop having sex with him, but I was afraid he wouldn't understand. In order to ignore my complicated feelings, I went back to the trick that kept me sane during the abuse: I detached my mind from my body.

I would tune in to the first time we met when he was just another face and remember how, after five years, he started showing interest in me and we began dating. I would romance about our relationship in my mind as if everything was going great between us, just to get through.

I don't know if the flashbacks led us to have problems, or if I started having the flashbacks because we were already in conflict. Whatever the case, we were having conflicts about control, and for me to be able to stand having sex, I have to be in control.

It's been six years since the judge granted me an order of protection from my father, but any reminder of his presence still alarms me. Memories of the abuse he put me through haunt me.

Sometimes I get nightmares and wake up in a cold sweat in the middle of the night, or I get flashbacks when I'm in the shower or when I'm rubbing lotion against my skin. I feel really nervous and uncomfortable touching myself in even these minor ways because painful memories come back.

I remember one dreary evening waking up to the heavy scent of tobacco (my father was a smoker), though no one was in the house at the time. I felt his presence nearby.

My skin began to crawl and horrible feelings of my father depriving me of my childhood tormented me all over again. I cried, holding my underwear tightly against my skin. I wanted my virginity back.

I hated him for abusing his role as a father. He was supposed to be a male figure that I could trust and turn to. I hated my sexuality. I was angry at the world for what had happened to me.

When I became a teenager, memories of the abuse led me to grow protective of my body. I hated getting attention from men. I kept myself covered up to avoid any boys piercing their eyes at me.

When shopping for clothes, I made sure that nothing I bought was too revealing. No v-neck blouses, spaghetti straps, halter tops or short skirts. I would be the only fool wearing a black denim jacket while roasting in 90 degree weather. I feared that by attracting attention from men I would be putting myself in danger. I was very cautious about the message I was sending.

When Kevin and I started dating, he was shy and very respectful. I'd never met anyone like him before. It took him months to have the courage to kiss me.

He also gave me full control over our relationship, which was something I wasn't always used to. At times I would yell at him just because I could, and he would start crying. He'd get worried when he did things to upset me. I smiled at this advantage behind closed doors. It felt good playing the dominant role in a relationship. I teased him and made him feel guilty if I didn't get my way.

I did these things because a part of me wanted revenge. I felt every man deserved the mighty strike of a woman's wrath. All my life I'd been surrounded by male figures like my father and uncles who would physically and sexually abuse and control their wives and, in my father's case, his children, too.

When I became a teenager, I hated getting attention from men.

Eventually, Kevin caught on to the idea that I was taking advantage of him and grew tired of me always having things my way. He wanted me to stop walking all over him, so he started to yell and argue with me. But I was so fearful of losing control that I was willing to fight for my advantage.

Many times when I felt Kevin was trying to take over, I would get nervous and show off by proving to him who was boss. When I yelled at Kevin, I was yelling at him and my father—any man who tried to manipulate me.

Soon we were arguing non-stop. On the phone, especially, we exchanged curses and insults. Sometimes he'd just explode in the street, yelling as if I was deaf. One time he ended up breaking his cellular phone in half because he was so angry with me.

Deep dow we were both trying to prove something to one another. Kevin was also in foster care, abandoned by his mother, and our relationship probably raised fears in him, too, that neither one of us could understand. We were driving each other nuts.

Without feeling in control of our relationship, I could no longer feel comfortable having sex. But I didn't tell Kevin because I didn't think he would ever understand. I wasn't even sure that I understood what I was feeling.

I especially didn't want him to feel uneasy and worried around me, or to feel like I was accusing him of abusing me. I just wanted our relationship to feel the way it used to. I figured that my feelings would soon pass. Unfortunately, they didn't.

I felt like a victim, taunted by my past. I hated feeling that way. Trying to hide how I felt, I sometimes ended up drinking to make it easier for me to not feel ashamed of doing things I didn't want to do. Then, after a while, I started to feel like I didn't care anymore about how I felt. I found myself saying, "All that matters is that Kevin loves me."

I wasn't sure what was going on with me. I had no grip. I'd lost the control I had longed for. And what had happened to my values and my self-esteem?

*P*lenty of times I wanted out, but I felt I'd be lost without him in my life. At around that time, my sister and grandmother were both hospitalized for mental illness, and I was moved into a strange new foster home where no one cared about me and I had little contact with family or friends. I felt vulnerable and lonely. Kevin kept me company and gave me support. But with no one else to lean on, I grew too dependent on him.

I thought to myself, "Can Kevin and I find a way to be together without our pasts getting in the way?"

I tried to be careful of the things I said around him to avoid the arguments, but sometimes I felt I had no choice but to go off.

I told myself, "I refuse to repeat my childhood and accept disrespect from anyone."

I guess Kevin felt the same way. He was just as concerned about getting his point across.

After two years, he announced that he wanted "a break." As much as I'd often longed for the same thing, I was furious and desperate. I spent hours over the phone trying to convince him to come back, but my pleas weren't enough.

After several days, I figured I would win Kevin back by having sex with him again. That night, we both ended up drinking heavily—maybe because we both felt uncomfortable—and had sex. I felt miserable afterwards because Kevin didn't immediately want to get back together. He said he still had feelings for me but the arguments were too much for him.

I'm trying hard to separate the past from the present. Kevin isn't my father.

We decided to try to work things out, but to take things a bit more slowly. We both want to rebuild our trust in each other and stop fighting for control. I would like Kevin to be more considerate of my feelings and to understand that it hasn't been easy coping with my past experience, and I would like to be able to do the same for him.

I'm trying hard to separate the past from the present. Kevin isn't my father. Though we argue, Kevin does not intend to do harm to me. I need to stop exploding at every argument we have. Kevin and I have been together for a long time, and I'm hopeful that we can both be more understanding and patient.

Lately, Kevin and I have been doing a lot of talking and hanging out and going to the movies. We've found lots of other activities to do together rather than have sex. I enjoy the time we're spending together because we're learning more new things about one another, and I don't have to feel pressure to have sex. I'm happy with the way things are now. I would like our relationship to remain this way until I feel ready for sex.

I am aware that it may be a long time until I can recover from the abuse I went through. But I can also see how far I've come. I used to fear and hate all men. Now I date and socialize with them. I am learning that some men, including Kevin, can be trusted.

I have to stop taking my anger out on Kevin, and I have to try not to control him. I hope he can do the same for me.

The author was 19 when she wrote this story.
She later enrolled in college to study social work.

Rikou Takatoshi / Stephanie Wilson

Leaving the Abuse Behind

Dr. Sylvia Lester, a psychologist in New York City, explains what it takes to recover from sexual abuse.

Q: How can sexual abuse repeat itself in your life?

A: Once you've been sexually abused, I think you are at a greater risk for being abused again, for many reasons. One is that quality of familiarity. We always look for what's familiar to us. It's almost like an addiction to helplessness, because that feeling of being helpless is so familiar.

On the other hand, the idea of being helpless is something that we all hate, so often victims will try to turn it around and do things that make them feel in control. Sometimes victims will develop eating disorders, because that's about having control over your body and what happens to it. Or they'll become promiscuous or even sexually abuse others.

They might become self-destructive in any number of ways. The idea is that now you're choosing to do this, and you're the powerful one. I think that's hard to get away from. But very often what happens is you do stuff and you think it's by choice but then it makes you feel helpless and ashamed. So you're actually getting yourself back into the cycle of bad feelings that you thought you were choosing to not go into.

You really can be doing things that make you feel helpless and in control at the same time. It's very hard to break the pattern of shame and feeling unsafe.

Q: What happens if you don't deal with the abuse?

A: If you don't deal with sexual abuse, it will keep coming up for you in some way. Just because you're not thinking of it all the time doesn't mean it's gone. It's almost like a virus.

Sometimes it comes up in a pattern of unsafe behaviors, like those I mentioned. Other times it comes up in flashbacks (when you experience a past event so vividly it's as if you're reliving it). Even years later, flashbacks are a sign that the trauma is still active, and you need help with it.

Flashbacks are a sign that the trauma is still active, and you need help with it.

What you want to do is sort of defuse it so it can become a memory but doesn't have the reality of being in the same situation again and again with all the same feelings and bodily reactions. This stuff sits in us and anything can trigger it, like pushing a button, and all of those feelings become alive. That really needs to be addressed for it to go away.

Even if the abuse doesn't come into your thoughts in a constant kind of way, it can repeat itself generationally, in your own kids. In most cases, a parent who has failed to protect their child from abuse is someone who herself was abused and never dealt with it.

Q: How can you break the cycle?

A: The first thing is to find a person that you can tell, who will actually respond, and who will not make you feel ashamed—it's almost as if you need to find a person who will feel the outrage that it would have been appropriate for a parent to feel. Someone's got to acknowledge and want to protect the victim and help them find safety.

But it's very common that either someone doesn't believe you or they blame you for it. And that makes it much harder to tell somebody else. It's very important to believe yourself no matter what anybody says and believes that this was something bad that happened to you. Even if you're out of the situation the other real piece of trauma is that you haven't been believed. That's a whole other thing to deal with.

Survivors of sexual abuse don't have a way of trusting their judgment about who will keep them safe. That's a learning process.

Q: Where can you get help?

A: There are a lot of places out there to get help. Looking for a place where the abuse can be spoken about is really important. There are self-help groups for survivors of incest or any sexual abuse. There's also individual therapy, and treatments like hypnosis.

In cases of sexual abuse, the victim is never seen. To recover, they have to figure out how they can get themselves seen and acknowledged, as people. They need to be with other people who can look at them and recognize them. After being abused it's like they go into hiding, so the work is to come out of hiding, in a way. That work needs a safe place, a therapy where you can feel accepted and acceptable.

Q: Why is it so difficult to recover from sexual abuse?

A: For kids who get abused, what doesn't get developed is the feeling that you have a choice. Somebody else is more powerful and there's no choice around it. To develop a sense of having a choice is a hard thing.

I think the other thing is that people don't have just one feeling about this. Very often an abusive relationship can be with someone who you do feel loved by or who you admire.

There may be something good about it, or at least it may feel that way in the beginning, so it's a complicated thing. There can be a certain amount of helplessness but excitement at the same time. You might be scared but like the attention. That's why it's so hard to break the cycle—it's hard to disentangle when there's more than one feeling.

Q: How long does it take to recover?

A: It's hard to say. I think it is a process, and some people spend their whole lives repeating abusive relationships or staying out of relationships because they can't stay safe. It really is almost like dealing with an addiction.

To develop the ability to protect yourself takes work. Survivors of sexual abuse don't have a way of trusting their judgment about who will keep them safe. That's a learning process.

It takes a certain amount of work and a certain amount of looking for people who may be unfamiliar—people who can care for you and be careful with you. Talk therapy also helps. It takes courage to talk about what have been secret and painful experiences. The pain may be hidden in what we do, in our bodies, but we need to listen for it and make sure we are with others who listen too.

Where to Get Help

You can find information and search for a counseling center near you on the RAINN (Rape, Abuse and Incest National Network) website: www.rainn.org

Or call their hotline:
1-800-656-HOPE

Townsend Press

Summer of Secrets

"I can't do this again, Carl. I don't have the strength, not without Mama."

Darcy Wills hid in the dark hallway listening to the sound of her mother's weary voice. It was 11:00 at night, and Mom was in the bedroom talking with Dad. Their door was closed. But through the thin walls of her family's small house, Darcy could hear them as if they were standing right in front of her.

"So what are you trying to say?" Dad asked. His voice was strained, as if he was carrying a heavy block of cement on his back.

Darcy stood still as a statue, careful not to make a sound that would alert her parents to the fact that she was just a few feet away in the dark.

"I don't know, Carl," Mom answered.

"I don't know anything anymore."

There was a moment of silence, and Darcy thought she heard

This is the first chapter from *Summer of Secrets*, by Paul Langan, a novel about teens facing difficult situations like the ones you read about in this book. *Summer of Secrets* is one of many books in the Bluford Series™ by Townsend Press.

her mother sob.

"I just don't have a good feeling about any of this."

So it was true, Darcy thought. Something was definitely wrong with her parents. Darcy had sensed it for days. She had noticed tension between them and had even heard Mom snap a few times, but until now she figured her mother was still recovering from the loss of Grandma.

Only three weeks ago, after a slow, steady decline in her health, Grandma had died in her sleep in the bedroom at the end of the hallway. The loss left a depressing void in the house. But in the three weeks that had passed, the sadness was replaced by an uncomfortable silence, one Darcy couldn't understand.

"Just don't worry about it, Darce," said her sister Jamee last week. Jamee was fourteen, two years younger than Darcy. "Anyway, it's none of your business. Besides, Mom's tough, and Dad's here. They'll be okay."

Darcy had rolled her eyes at her sister's comment. Jamee wasn't the best person to judge a situation. Only six months ago, she had dated Bobby Wallace, a sixteen-year-old who messed with drugs, hit Jamee, and convinced her to shoplift for him.

"How can you be so sure?" Darcy had asked.

Jamee shrugged off the question. "You know what your problem is, Darcy? You think too much," she said and then left to go to the movies with her friend Cindy Gibson. It was what Jamee always did when anything serious confronted her. Run away. Hide. Ignore it. Anything to avoid things that were unpleasant or difficult. It was Jamee's way, not Darcy's.

No, the problem is that you don't think enough, Darcy thought as she watched her sister leave. No matter what Jamee said, Darcy knew the issue with her parents was serious. For weeks, Mom had walked around in a daze, sometimes, it seemed, on the verge of tears.

Yesterday, Darcy even spotted her watching what she hated most—a TV show about a hospital emergency room. For as long as Darcy could remember, Mom had forbidden all medical shows when she was around.

"I see that stuff every day at work. I'm not going to watch it when I'm home," she had once declared. Mom was an emergency room nurse. Though she rarely discussed what she saw at the hospital, Darcy knew that her mother witnessed victims of shootings, stabbings, car accidents, and all sorts of diseases. No wonder she didn't want to see it on TV. But last night, she did not even seem to notice the TV doctors trying to revive a patient who had a heart attack. It was as if her mind was somewhere else. As if she wasn't in the room, even though her body was sprawled across the couch.

But tonight, Mom was even worse. Her face looked worn when she came home from the hospital. It wasn't the usual tiredness that made her stretch out on the couch and sleep after she got home. It was deeper, as if Mom's spirit was drained like an old battery.

"Are you all right?" Darcy had asked as Mom came in the front door, slumped onto the living room sofa, and sighed. She had not even said hello to Dad, who was making dinner for her in the kitchen.

"I'm fine," Mom grumbled. Her voice had a hollow sound to it, as if she didn't believe her own words.

Darcy was certain her parents were having serious problems. That had to be why Mom was acting so strange. The last time Darcy had witnessed her parents fighting was when she was in middle school, just before her father left. There was the same tension in the house then, the same awkward silence.

"Are you sure you're okay, Mom?" Darcy had asked, hoping her mother would explain what was bothering her. Darcy couldn't help remembering the August day years ago when Dad took her and Jamee out for ice cream. She recalled the pained look on his face and the heavy drag of his steps on the concrete. It was the last thing he did with them before he took off, before the five-year span without a phone call, a birthday card, or a single word.

Mom cried every night for a month when Dad left. Seeing her so upset was almost worse than losing Dad. It was a kind of torture that made Darcy shudder whenever she remembered it. Only Grandma's strength enabled Mom to work full time, pay the bills, and hold the family together. Now Grandma was gone, and Darcy knew that if her parents split up again, there would be no one for Mom to turn to.

"Yes, I'm sure!" Mom snapped. "I'm just tired. You understand? And you know the one thing that bothers me most when I'm tired? It's people asking me what's wrong."

"Sorry," Darcy said, stepping back. She had not expected Mom to get so angry. It was just more proof that there were major problems in the family.

For the rest of the evening, Mom didn't say a word, even when Jamee came home a half hour late from the movies.

"Cindy's mom was late picking us up," Jamee explained as soon as she walked in.

Darcy did not believe her sister. There was something rehearsed about what she said, as if she had practiced it a few times. But Mom didn't even acknowledge Jamee, who quickly grabbed the cordless phone from the kitchen and retreated into her room.

For two hours, except for the TV, everything was unnaturally quiet. But Darcy knew it was a false calm, like the muffled silence just before a bad storm.

As soon as her parents headed into the bedroom, Darcy turned out the lights, locked the doors, and crept into the hallway to find out what was wrong. Now she stood outside her parents' bedroom, trying to catch pieces of their private conversation.

"What can I say to make you feel better about this?" Dad said. Darcy could feel the strain in his voice. He was upset.

"There's nothing you can say," Mom replied. "I'm too old for this, and I don't want to be in this situation. I just can't do it again, Carl. I just can't."

Suddenly Jamee's bedroom door opened, and she stepped into the hallway. Darcy turned and tried to act as if she was walking toward her own bedroom.

"What are you doing?" Jamee whispered, nearly running into Darcy.

"Just going to bed."

"No you're not. You're listening to Mom and Dad, aren't you?" "*No*," Darcy whispered. "And keep your voice down."

"Darcy, you're the worst liar. Even in the dark, I can tell you aren't telling the truth. Why don't you just leave them alone?"

"Because something is wrong , Jamee. I know it. They didn't say a word to each other at dinner tonight, and even you had to notice that Mom's been out of it. I'm just worried."

"Maybe she's just in a bad mood or something," Jamee said, but her whisper cracked. Darcy could see Jamee's eyes dart back and forth in the darkness. She was shaking her head the way she always did when she was upset.

Though Jamee talked tough, Darcy knew that her younger sister looked up to Dad more than anyone in the world. Jamee would take it harder than anyone if Mom and Dad were having problems.

"I hope that's all it is, Jamee," Darcy said, though she was sure it wasn't. And she suspected Jamee felt the same way.

Jamee walked into the kitchen, hung up the phone she had grabbed earlier, and poured herself a glass of water. Darcy followed her.

"Why can't things just be easy for once?" Jamee said, leaning against the kitchen wall.

The two were silent for a second. Darcy wished Grandma was there to talk to. Or that Hakeem, her ex-boyfriend, was somewhere nearby so she could call him. But Grandma was gone, dead from a massive stroke, and Hakeem was living in

Detroit, far away f rom their crowded neighborhood in southern California.

"I don't wanna think about something bad happening with Mom and Dad. I just can't deal with that," Jamee confessed between sips of water.

"Like you said. Maybe it's not that bad," Darcy replied, trying to keep her sister's spirits up.

"Yeah right," Jamee whispered bitterly. "When are things around here ever better than you expected?"

Before Darcy could reply, her sister turned and walked out of the kitchen. "I'm going to bed," Jamee said as she left. A second later, her bedroom door closed with a soft thud.

Darcy stood at the edge of the dark hallway and listened.

The house was deathly quiet, as if everything had been swept under a heavy blanket of gloom. Reluctantly, she decided to go to bed too.

Lying in bed, Darcy stared at the shadowy ceiling of her room, unable to relax. It was so quiet she could hear the rhythmic click of her watch on the other side of the room.

Tick tick tick. Like the heartbeat of some unwanted guest.

Darcy's body was tired from a full day of work at Scoops, the new ice cream parlor not far from Bluford High, where she had just finished her sophomore year. But her mind was wide awake, as if she had just drunk ten cups of coffee.

It had been this way for days, even before she noticed the strange tension between her parents. As soon as it got quiet and she was ready to go to sleep, Darcy would remember the afternoon weeks ago, when she was attacked by Brian Mason.

Often the memory was so strong, it was as if he was in the room with her, pinning her down, threatening her again, making her heart race with fear.

"What's wrong with you?" Brian's words still insulted her, bouncing inside her mind like ricocheting bullets. When he attacked, Darcy had struggled to free herself, but Brian's grip

was strong, like a vise crushing her arm. Sometimes, she still felt the pain from where he had pinned her against the couch in his apartment. "Stop it!" she had demanded. "Let me go."

It had been a nightmare that caught Darcy completely off-guard. She had met Brian just before summer vacation began when she babysat for his sister, Liselle. At first, he seemed nice, and for a time, Darcy was flattered by his attention, especially after her old boyfriend, Hakeem Randall, broke up with her. On the day of the attack, Brian invited her to spend time alone with him, and she agreed, lying to her parents so they would let her out. But once she got there, Brian started getting physical with her. Too physical.

"You're acting like a baby," Brian had yelled when Darcy tried to stop him from lifting up her shirt.

Darcy could still feel him gripping her, his wet lips pushing against her neck, his roving hands. His musky smell. On that afternoon, he had touched her more than any other boy, even Hakeem.

No one except Mom and Dad knew of the attack. Not Jamee. Not Hakeem. Not even Tarah Carson, Darcy's best friend. It was a secret, an invisible scar Darcy faced alone each night.

If Dad hadn't shown up . . .

Darcy could not bear the thought, yet she couldn't escape it either. She knew the dark corner it went to. It was the same conclusion every night.

In fifth grade, just before Dad left, Darcy had gotten into a fight at school with a seventh grade boy who pulled her bra strap, making it snap painfully against her back. To the kid, it was just a joke. But Dad had seen what happened, grabbed the boy and dragged him to the principal's office.

"What's wrong with you, boy? You treat girls with respect, you hear me!" Dad had yelled, holding the kid's shirt in his clenched fist. Even the principal looked scared.

It was then Darcy knew her father would always keep her

safe. Would protect her when she needed it. Would never allow anyone to hurt her. Dad had proved that again when Brian attacked. He had saved her. He had stopped Brian from going any further. He had found her and brought her home.

But now, with her parents fighting, it seemed Dad might not always be there. Maybe he would go away again, perhaps for good. Darcy trembled in her bed.

If Dad hadn't shown up . . .

If Dad wasn't there . . .

If Dad leaves again . . .

Darcy's mind raced, as it had each night for the past week. In the shadows, she could almost feel the specter of Brian watching her. And even though she knew he was gone, that he had moved over 300 miles away to Oakland to live with his aunt, Darcy still could not shake the damage he had done, the crack he had put in her world, one that left voices deep inside her which she could not silence.

"You're not safe," the voices said. *"Boys can't be trusted. The world is dangerous. Your father won't always be there to protect you."*

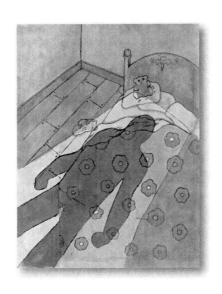

Teens:
How to Get More Out of This Book

Self-help: The teens who wrote the stories in this book did so because they hope that telling their stories will help readers who are facing similar challenges. They want you to know that you are not alone, and that taking specific steps can help you manage or overcome very difficult situations. They've done their best to be clear about the actions that worked for them so you can see if they'll work for you.

Writing: You can also use the book to improve your writing skills. Each teen in this book wrote 5-10 drafts of his or her story before it was published. If you read the stories closely you'll see that the teens work to include a beginning, a middle, and an end, and good scenes, description, dialogue, and anecdotes (little stories). To improve your writing, take a look at how these writers construct their stories. Try some of their techniques in your own writing.

Reading: Finally, you'll notice that we include the first chapter from a Bluford Series novel in this book, alongside the true stories by teens. We hope you'll like it enough to continue reading. The more you read, the more you'll strengthen your reading skills. Teens at Youth Communication like the Bluford novels because they explore themes similar to those in their own stories. Your school may already have the Bluford books. If not, you can order them online for only $1.

Resources on the Web

We will occasionally post Think About It questions on our website, www.youthcomm.org, to accompany stories in this and other Youth Communication books. We try out the questions with teens and post the ones they like best. Many teens report that writing answers to those questions in a journal is very helpful.

How to Use This Book in Staff Training

Staff say that reading these stories gives them greater insight into what teens are thinking and feeling, and new strategies for working with them. You can help the staff you work with by using these stories as case studies.

Select one story to read in the group, and ask staff to identify and discuss the main issue facing the teen. There may be disagreement about this, based on the background and experience of staff. That is fine. One point of the exercise is that teens have complex lives and needs. Adults can probably be more effective if they don't focus too narrowly and can see several dimensions of their clients.

Ask staff: What issues or feelings does the story provoke in them? What kind of help do they think the teen wants? What interventions are likely to be most promising? Least effective? Why? How would you build trust with the teen writer? How have other adults failed the teen, and how might that affect his or her willingness to accept help? What other resources would be helpful to this teen, such as peer support, a mentor, counseling, family therapy, etc.

Resources on the Web

From time to time we will post Think About It questions on our website, www.youthcomm.org, to accompany stories in this and other Youth Communication books. We try out the questions with teens and post the ones that they find most effective. We'll also post lesson for some of the stories. Adults can use the questions and lessons in workshops.

Teachers and Staff:
How to Use This Book in Groups

When working with teens individually or in groups, using these stories can help young people face difficult issues in a way that feels safe to them. That's because talking about the issues in the stories usually feels safer to teens than talking about those same issues in their own lives. Addressing issues through the stories allows for some personal distance; they hit close to home, but not too close. Talking about them opens up a safe place for reflection. As teens gain confidence talking about the issues in the stories, they usually become more comfortable talking about those issues in their own lives.

Below are general questions that can help you lead discussions about the stories, which help teens and staff reflect on the issues in their own work and lives. In most cases you can read a story and conduct a discussion in one 45-minute session. Teens are usually happy to read the stories aloud, with each teen reading a paragraph or two. (Allow teens to pass if they don't want to read.) It takes 10-15 minutes to read a story straight through. However, it is often more effective to let workshop participants make comments and discuss the story as you go along. The workshop leader may even want to annotate her copy of the story beforehand with key questions.

If teens read the story ahead of time or silently, it's good to break the ice with a few questions that get everyone on the same page: Who is the main character? How old is she? What happened to her? How did she respond? Etc. Another good starting question is: "What stood out for you in the story?" Go around the room and let each person briefly mention one thing.

Then move on to open-ended questions, which encourage participants to think more deeply about what the writers were feeling, the choices they faced, and they actions they took. There are no right or wrong answers to the open-ended questions. Open-ended questions encourage participants to think about how the themes, emotions and choices in the stories relate to their own lives. Here are some examples of open-ended questions that we have found to be effective. You can use variations of these questions with almost any story in this book.

—What main problem or challenge did the writer face?

—What choices did the teen have in trying to deal with the problem?

—Which way of dealing with the problem was most effective for the teen? Why?

—What strengths, skills, or resources did the teen use to address the challenge?

—If you were in the writer's shoes, what would you have done?

—What could adults have done better to help this young person?

—What have you learned by reading this story that you didn't know before?

—What, if anything, will you do differently after reading this story?

—What surprised you in this story?

—Do you have a different view of this issue, or see a different way of dealing with it, after reading this story? Why or why not?

Credits

The stories in this book originally appeared in the following Youth Communication publications:

"I'm Glad I Spoke Up," by Anonymous, *Represent*, March/April 1999

"Haunted," by Anonymous, *Represent*, July/August 2000

"I'm Sorry: A Sex Offender Speaks Out," by Anonymous, *Represent*, July/August 2000

"Eyes Wide Shut," by Anonymous, *Represent*, May/June 2002

"When Loved Ones Don't Listen," by Anonymous, *Represent*, May/June 2002

"Not Yet," by T. Mahdi, *Represent*, October/November 2006

"Alone with My Abuser," by Anonymous, *New Youth Connections*, April 2009

"Missing His Harmful, Hurting Hands," by Anonymous, *Represent*, September/October 2004

"A Partner in His Crime?" by Anonymous, *Represent*, November/December 2000

"Facing the Truth," *Rise*, Fall 2007

"Making It Out," *Represent*, January/February 2007

"Painting My Way Through," by Aquellah Mahdi, *Represent*, November/December 2005

"Speaking Up," by Akeema Lottman, *Represent*, July/August 2008

"Trying to Bury the Past," *Represent*, January/February 2007

"Leaving the Abuse Behind," *Represent*, January/February 2007

About
Youth Communication

Youth Communication, founded in 1980, is a nonprofit youth development program located in New York City whose mission is to teach writing, journalism, and leadership skills. The teenagers we train become writers for our websites and books and for two print magazines, *New Youth Connections*, a general-interest youth magazine, and *Represent*, a magazine by and for young people in foster care.

Each year, up to 100 young people participate in Youth Communication's school-year and summer journalism workshops where they work under the direction of full-time professional editors. Most are African American, Latino, or Asian, and many are recent immigrants. The opportunity to reach their peers with accurate portrayals of their lives and important self-help information motivates the young writers to create powerful stories.

Our goal is to run a strong youth development program in which teens produce high quality stories that inform and inspire their peers. Doing so requires us to be sensitive to the complicated lives and emotions of the teen participants while also providing an intellectually rigorous experience. We achieve that goal in the writing/teaching/editing relationship, which is the core of our program.

Our teaching and editorial process begins with discussions

between adult editors and the teen staff. In those meetings, the teens and the editors work together to identify the most important issues in the teens' lives and to figure out how those issues can be turned into stories that will resonate with teen readers.

Once story topics are chosen, students begin the process of crafting their stories. For a personal story, that means revisiting events in one's past to understand their significance for the future. For a commentary, it means developing a logical and persuasive point of view. For a reported story, it means gathering information through research and interviews. Students look inward and outward as they try to make sense of their experiences and the world around them and find the points of intersection between personal and social concerns. That process can take a few weeks or a few months. Stories frequently go through ten or more drafts as students work under the guidance of their editors, the way any professional writer does.

Many of the students who walk through our doors have uneven skills, as a result of poor education, living under extremely stressful conditions, or coming from homes where English is a second language. Yet, to complete their stories, students must successfully perform a wide range of activities, including writing and rewriting, reading, discussion, reflection, research, interviewing, and typing. They must work as members of a team and they must accept individual responsibility. They learn to provide constructive criticism, and to accept it. They engage in explorations of truthfulness, fairness, and accuracy. They meet deadlines. They must develop the audacity to believe that they have something important to say and the humility to recognize that saying it well is not a process of instant gratification. Rather, it usually requires a long, hard struggle through many discussions and much rewriting.

It would be impossible to teach these skills and dispositions as separate, disconnected topics, like grammar, ethics, or assertiveness. However, we find that students make rapid progress when they are learning skills in the context of an inquiry that is personally significant to them and that will benefit their peers.

When teens publish their stories—in *New Youth Connections* and *Represent*, on the web, and in other publications—they reach tens of thousands of teen and adult readers. Teachers, counselors, social workers, and other adults circulate the stories to young people in their classes and out-of-school youth programs. Adults tell us that teens in their programs—including many who are ordinarily resistant to reading—clamor for the stories. Teen readers report that the stories give them information they can't get anywhere else, and inspire them to reflect on their lives and open lines of communication with adults.

Writers usually participate in our program for one semester, though some stay much longer. Years later, many of them report that working here was a turning point in their lives—that it helped them acquire the confidence and skills that they needed for success in college and careers. Scores of our graduates have overcome tremendous obstacles to become journalists, writers, and novelists. They include National Book Award finalist Edwidge Danticat, novelist Ernesto Quinonez, writer Veronica Chambers and *New York Times* reporter Rachel Swarns. Hundreds more are working in law, business, and other careers. Many are teachers, principals, and youth workers, and several have started nonprofit youth programs themselves and work as mentors— helping another generation of young people develop their skills and find their voices.

Youth Communication is a nonprofit educational corporation. Contributions are gratefully accepted and are tax deductible to the fullest extent of the law.

To make a contribution, or for information about our publications and programs, including our catalog of over 100 books and curricula for hard-to-reach teens, see www.youthcomm.org

About The Editors

Al Desetta has been an editor of Youth Communication's two teen magazines, *Foster Care Youth United* (now known as *Represent*) and *New Youth Connections*. He was also an instructor in Youth Communication's juvenile prison writing program. In 1991, he became the organization's first director of teacher development, working with high school teachers to help them produce better writers and student publications.

Prior to working at Youth Communication, Desetta directed environmental education projects in New York City public high schools and worked as a reporter.

He has a master's degree in English literature from City College of the City University of New York and a bachelor's degree from the State University of New York at Binghamton, and he was a Revson Fellow at Columbia University for the 1990-91 academic year.

He is the editor of many books, including several other Youth Communication anthologies: *The Heart Knows Something Different: Teenage Voices from the Foster Care System, The Struggle to Be Strong,* and *The Courage to Be Yourself.* He is currently a freelance editor.

Keith Hefner co-founded Youth Communication in 1980 and has directed it ever since. He is the recipient of the Luther P. Jackson Education Award from the New York Association of Black Journalists and a MacArthur Fellowship. He was also a Revson Fellow at Columbia University.

Laura Longhine is the editorial director at Youth Communication. She edited *Represent*, Youth Communication's magazine by and for youth in foster care, for three years, and has written for a variety of publications. She has a BA in English from Tufts University and an MS in Journalism from Columbia University.

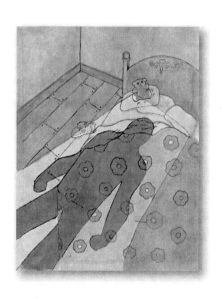

More Helpful Books
From Youth Comunication

 *The Struggle to Be Strong: True Stories by Teens About Overcoming Tough Times.* Foreword by Veronica Chambers. Help young people identify and build on their own strengths with 30 personal stories about resiliency. (Free Spirit)

Fighting the Monster: Teens Write About Confronting Emotional Challenges and Getting Help. Introduction by Dr. Francine Cournos. Teens write about their struggle to achieve emotional well-being. Topics include: Cutting, depression, bereavement, substance abuse, and more. (Youth Communication)

 Depression, Anger, Sadness: Teens Write About Facing Difficult Emotions. Give teens the confidence they need to seek help when they need it. These teens write candidly about difficult emotional problems—such as depression, cutting, and domestic violence—and how they have tried to help themselves. (Youth Communication)

My Secret Addiction: Teens Write About Cutting. These true accounts of cutting, or self-mutilation, offer a window into the personal and family situations that lead to this secret habit, and show how teens can get the help they need. (Youth Communication)

 *Enjoy the Moment: Teens Write About Dealing With Stress.* Help decrease the levels of stress and conflict in your teens' lives. These young writers describe how they cope with stress, using methods including meditation, journal writing, and exercise. (Youth Communication)

 *The Fury Inside: Teens Write About Anger.* Help teens manage their anger. These writers tell how they got better control of their emotions and sought the support of others. (Youth Communication)

Analyze This: Teens Write About Therapy. Get insight into how therapy looks from a teen's perspective and help teens find the services they need. Teens in foster care write about their experiences with therapy. Some are happy with the help, while others are dissatisfied or confused. (Youth Communication)

 Putting the Pieces Together Again: Teens Write About Surviving Rape. These stories show how teens have coped with the nightmare experience of rape and taken steps toward recovery. (Youth Communication)

Sticks and Stones: Teens Write About Bullying. Shed light on bullying, as told from the perspectives of the perpetrator, the victim, and the witness. These stories show why bullying occurs, the harm it causes, and how it might be prevented. (Youth Communication)

 Out With It: Gay and Straight Teens Write About Homosexuality. Break stereotypes and provide support with this unflinching look at gay life from a teen's perspective. With a focus on urban youth, this book also includes several heterosexual teens' transformative experiences with gay peers. (Youth Communication)

To order these and other books, go to:
www.youthcomm.org
or call 212-279-0708 x115

LaVergne, TN USA
11 April 2010
178892LV00002B/117/P

9 781933 939810